SpringerBriefs in Economics

SpringerBriefs present concise summaries of cutting-edge research and practical applications across a wide spectrum of fields. Featuring compact volumes of 50 to 125 pages, the series covers a range of content from professional to academic. Typical topics might include:

- A timely report of state-of-the art analytical techniques
- A bridge between new research results, as published in journal articles, and a contextual literature review
- A snapshot of a hot or emerging topic
- An in-depth case study or clinical example
- A presentation of core concepts that students must understand in order to make independent contributions

SpringerBriefs in Economics showcase emerging theory, empirical research, and practical application in microeconomics, macroeconomics, economic policy, public finance, econometrics, regional science, and related fields, from a global author community.

Briefs are characterized by fast, global electronic dissemination, standard publishing contracts, standardized manuscript preparation and formatting guidelines, and expedited production schedules.

More information about this series at https://link.springer.com/bookseries/8876

Shoko Haneda · Arito Ono

R&D Management Practices and Innovation: Evidence from a Firm Survey

Shoko Haneda
Faculty of Commerce
Chuo University
Tokyo, Japan

Arito Ono
Faculty of Commerce
Chuo University
Tokyo, Japan

ISSN 2191-5504　　　　　　　ISSN 2191-5512　(electronic)
SpringerBriefs in Economics
ISBN 978-981-16-9796-8　　　ISBN 978-981-16-9797-5　(eBook)
https://doi.org/10.1007/978-981-16-9797-5

© The Author(s) 2022. This book is an open access publication.

Open Access This book is licensed under the terms of the Creative Commons Attribution 4.0 International License (http://creativecommons.org/licenses/by/4.0/), which permits use, sharing, adaptation, distribution and reproduction in any medium or format, as long as you give appropriate credit to the original author(s) and the source, provide a link to the Creative Commons license and indicate if changes were made.

The images or other third party material in this book are included in the book's Creative Commons license, unless indicated otherwise in a credit line to the material. If material is not included in the book's Creative Commons license and your intended use is not permitted by statutory regulation or exceeds the permitted use, you will need to obtain permission directly from the copyright holder.

The use of general descriptive names, registered names, trademarks, service marks, etc. in this publication does not imply, even in the absence of a specific statement, that such names are exempt from the relevant protective laws and regulations and therefore free for general use.

The publisher, the authors and the editors are safe to assume that the advice and information in this book are believed to be true and accurate at the date of publication. Neither the publisher nor the authors or the editors give a warranty, expressed or implied, with respect to the material contained herein or for any errors or omissions that may have been made. The publisher remains neutral with regard to jurisdictional claims in published maps and institutional affiliations.

This Springer imprint is published by the registered company Springer Nature Singapore Pte Ltd.
The registered company address is: 152 Beach Road, #21-01/04 Gateway East, Singapore 189721, Singapore

Preface

This monograph provides a detailed account of what firms do in their R&D activities. In particular, using a unique survey of firms in Japan, we focus on the following four aspects of R&D management: the organizational structure of R&D, staged project management for R&D projects, compensation and incentive schemes for R&D personnel, and a firm's risk preferences and corporate culture. We also examine whether and how R&D management practices are linked to the likelihood of firms' success in making product innovations and the choice between explorative (radical) and exploitive (incremental) innovation.

While previous studies recognize that R&D management practices are important drivers of innovation, most take the form of case studies that focus on a particular aspect of R&D management, and there are few studies that systematically and quantitatively examine the link between various R&D management practices and innovation. To fill the gap in the literature, we designed and conducted the original firm survey, the "Survey of R&D Management Practices," in January–February 2020. This monograph presents our first step in examining how R&D management is associated with corporate innovation using the survey. We hope that this monograph is useful for readers interested in a detailed analysis of the relationship between R&D management and innovation using quantitative data.

This monograph is the product of a research project funded by a JSPS Grant-in-Aid for Scientific Research (B) No. 19H01488). We would like to thank an anonymous referee, Christian Rammer, Ralph Paprzycki, and participants of the 2021 Annual Meeting of the Japan Society for Research Policy and Innovation Management for their useful comments, Yuya Ikeda and Tomohiko Inui for conducting the survey with us, and Koki Kurihara for superb research assistance. We gratefully acknowledge the cooperation of the National Institute of Science and Technology Policy (NISTEP) in conducting the "Survey of R&D Management Practices." Ono gratefully acknowledges that this monograph was prepared while he was a visiting researcher at NISTEP, while Haneda acknowledges the hospitality she received while she was a visiting researcher at the ZEW (Leibniz Centre for European Economic Research).

Tokyo, Japan
Shoko Haneda
Arito Ono

Contents

1 **R&D Management Practices and Innovation: Evidence from a Firm Survey** 1
  1.1 Introduction 1
  1.2 Key Questions and Related Literature 2
      1.2.1 Organizational Structure of R&D Activities 3
      1.2.2 Staged Project Management 4
      1.2.3 Compensation and Incentive Schemes for R&D Personnel 7
      1.2.4 Risk Preferences and Corporate Culture 9
  1.3 Methodology 12
      1.3.1 Survey Design 12
      1.3.2 Summary Statistics 13
  1.4 R&D Outcomes and Inputs 15
      1.4.1 R&D Outcomes 15
      1.4.2 R&D Inputs: R&D Expenditures 19
          1.4.2.1 Amount of R&D Expenditure 19
          1.4.2.2 Funding Sources for R&D Expenditure 21
          1.4.2.3 Determinants of R&D Expenditure 23
      1.4.3 R&D Inputs: R&D Personnel 26
  1.5 Organizational Structure of R&D Activities 31
      1.5.1 Centralized/Decentralized R&D Structure 31
      1.5.2 Allocation of R&D Expenditure and R&D Personnel in Firms with a Hybrid R&D Structure 35
      1.5.3 Initiative in Hiring R&D Personnel 38
  1.6 R&D Project Management 40
      1.6.1 Overview on R&D Projects 40
          1.6.1.1 Number of R&D Projects 40
          1.6.1.2 Duration of R&D Projects 42
          1.6.1.3 Termination or Suspension of R&D Projects 42
      1.6.2 Staged Project Management 45
          1.6.2.1 Milestones 49

		1.6.2.2	Feedback	52
1.7	Evaluation of R&D Personnel			57
	1.7.1	Salary Schemes for R&D Personnel		57
	1.7.2	Performance- and Ability-Based Evaluation		61
		1.7.2.1	Weights on Performance and Ability in Evaluation	61
		1.7.2.2	Criteria for the Evaluation of R&D Personnel	62
	1.7.3	Incentive Schemes for R&D Personnel		65
	1.7.4	Incentives for Long-Term Success		69
		1.7.4.1	Rewards for Long-Term Success	69
		1.7.4.2	Possibility of Promotion	71
1.8	Risk Preferences and Corporate Culture			72
	1.8.1	Risk Preferences		72
	1.8.2	Corporate Culture		77
1.9	Conclusion			81

Appendix 85
Survey of R&D Management Practices 85
Glossary of Terms in the "Survey of R&D Management Practices" 94

References 97

About the Authors

Shoko Haneda is Professor at the Faculty of Commerce, Chuo University, Japan. She also served as visiting researcher at the National Institute of Science and Technology Policy (2011–2020). Her main fields of research are innovation, business economics, and management. She has published papers in *Research Policy*, *Economics of Innovation and New Technology*, and other scholarly journals. She received a B.A. in Mathematics from Tsuda University and a Ph.D. in Economics from Tsukuba University.

Arito Ono is Professor at the Faculty of Commerce, Chuo University, Japan. Prior to joining Chuo University in 2015, he was a senior economist at the Mizuho Research Institute, and a senior economist at the Institute for Monetary and Economic Studies, Bank of Japan (2009–2011). He also served as a member of several working groups at the Financial System Council, Financial Services Agency (2011–2015) and as an advisor at the Research and Statistics Department, Bank of Japan (2015). His main fields of research are banking and corporate finance. He is a coauthor and coeditor of the book titled *The Economics of Interfirm Networks* and has published academic articles in the *International Economic Review*, the *Journal of Banking & Finance*, the *Journal of Financial Stability*, the *Journal of Money, Credit, and Banking*, and *Real Estate Economics*, among others. He received a B.A. in economics from the University of Tokyo in 1991 and a Ph.D. in economics from Brown University in 2001.

Chapter 1
R&D Management Practices and Innovation: Evidence from a Firm Survey

1.1 Introduction

Innovation plays an important role in increasing productivity and economic growth. Much of this innovation is driven by the research and development (R&D) activities of business firms as part of their efforts to develop new products and processes. Against this background, how firms manage their R&D activities has become an increasingly important issue (see, e.g., Teece 1996; Azoulay and Lerner 2012). Meanwhile, there is a growing literature which argues that management practices are important factors in explaining differences in productivity across firms (e.g., Bloom and Van Reenen 2007, 2010; Bloom et al. 2019). Because innovation is a key determinant of a firm's productivity, this literature suggests that there is a link between R&D management practices, innovation, and productivity. Yet, while there are many case studies and small-sample studies describing how well-articulated R&D management practices create innovation (e.g., Hartmann and Hassan 2006; Hullova et al. 2019; Smolnik and Bergmann 2020), there are relatively few studies that empirically examine the link between R&D management practices and innovation using large-scale data (notable exceptions are Laursen and Foss 2003; Haneda and Ito 2018). Moreover, there are even fewer studies that systematically investigate from a variety of angles how firms manage R&D activities in practice and examine which R&D management practices are beneficial for, or detrimental to, innovation.

To fill the gap in the literature, this monograph seeks to better understand what firms do in their R&D activities using data from a unique survey of firms in Japan, the "Survey of R&D Management Practices," which was implemented by a research team including the authors in January–February 2020. This survey focuses on the following four aspects of R&D management: the organizational structure of R&D, staged project management for R&D projects, compensation and incentive schemes for R&D personnel, and a firm's risk preferences and corporate culture. Using an original data set that matches the survey data with firm-level micro data, we provide detailed information on firms' R&D management practices. We also examine whether and how various R&D management practices are linked to the likelihood of firms' success in making product innovations. Further, reflecting the fact that much of the literature on innovation focuses on the tension between explorative (radical) innovations and exploitative (incremental) innovations (e.g., March 1991; Manso 2011), we also investigate whether and how R&D management practices are associated with the choice between explorative and exploitative product innovation.

The remainder of this monograph is organized as follows. Section 1.2 explains the key question about R&D management practices asked in the survey and provides a review of the related literature motivating the questions. Section 1.3 outlines the survey design and presents basic summary statistics. Section 1.4 explains the variables we use for R&D outcomes and R&D inputs. Next, Sects. 1.5 to 1.8 are the main parts of this monograph. They provide detailed information on firms' R&D management practices, namely, on the organizational structure of R&D activities (Sect. 1.5), staged project management (Sect. 1.6), compensation and incentive schemes for R&D personnel (Sect. 1.7), and firms' risk preferences and corporate culture (Sect. 1.8). We also conduct a simple statistical analysis (two-sample equal variance t-tests) in these sections to examine the relationship between R&D management practices and R&D outcomes and discuss whether the results are consistent with the literature discussed in Sect. 1.2.[1] While we need to control for a range of factors such as firm size and industry to examine the link between R&D management practices and R&D outcomes more rigorously, we believe that our simple analysis serves as a useful first step for future studies. Section 1.9 concludes.

1.2 Key Questions and Related Literature

This section outlines the key questions about R&D management practices that we examine in this monograph. We formulate our key questions focusing on the following aspects: the organizational structure of R&D activities, staged projects management, compensation and incentive schemes for R&D personnel, and firms' risk preferences and corporate culture. We also review the related literature to which we refer in constructing these questions. In his seminal study, March (1991) argues that for many businesses innovation is difficult because there is a trade-off between allocating resources to the exploration of new possibilities and the exploitation of well-known approaches. The tension between exploration and exploitation is analyzed more formally by Manso (2011), who constructs a principal-agent model in which he embeds a Bayesian decision model known as the bandit problem. Manso (2011) shows that the optimal scheme for promoting innovation (exploration) is one that exhibits substantial tolerance for early failure, reward for long-term success, and timely feedback on performance. In formulating our key questions, we rely not only

---

[1] Note that our analyses are descriptive in nature and do not provide evidence of any causal relationships. While we discuss possible mechanisms that may explain our results, we do not formally test them, so that these discussions should be regarded as conjectures.

on the empirical implications of March's (1991) and Manso's (2011) analyses but also those of other studies that we discuss in detail below.

1.2.1 Organizational Structure of R&D Activities

Organizational economics theory suggests that a firm's internal organizational structure affects its performance (e.g., Gibbons and Roberts 2012). We examine how a firm's internal organizational structure of R&D activities affects its innovation from two separate but intertwined aspects. Specifically, we focus on how the delegation of authority to R&D organizations and the centralization or decentralization of R&D organization structures are linked with innovation outcomes.

First, to investigate the effect of delegation on innovation, we measure to what extent the authority to hire employees (R&D personnel) and to terminate/suspend or continue ongoing R&D projects is allocated between R&D organizations and corporate headquarters. Aghion and Tirole (1997) argue that the basic trade-off in delegating authority is between initiative and control. That is, the transfer of authority to an agent (an R&D organization in our case) increases the ability of the agent to take the initiative to acquire relevant knowledge for the project, but this comes at the expense of the principal's (the headquarters') control over the choice and management of projects. Aghion and Tirole's (1997) argument suggests that to what extent firms allocate authority to R&D organizations depends on whether their corporate headquarters have sufficient knowledge about choosing R&D personnel and running R&D projects. Consistent with Aghion and Tirole's (1997) prediction, Acemoglu et al. (2007) find that firms closer to the technological frontier are more likely to delegate authority to the manager (agent) of the firm's "profit center" business unit because there is less public information about the new technology from which corporate headquarters (the principal) can learn. Meanwhile, Kastl et al. (2013) empirically examine the link between delegation and R&D expenditure. Specifically, using a firm survey of Italian manufacturing firms, which asks a respondent firm whether R&D-related decisions, as well as administrative, financial, and business decisions, are autonomously made by separate divisions, they construct several measures of delegation. They find a positive correlation between the delegation measures and R&D expenditures, which suggests that firms in which more authority is delegated to the R&D division tend to spend more on R&D. In this study we measure the delegation of authority to hire researchers and manage on-going R&D projects to R&D organizations and examine the statistical association of such delegation with innovation outcomes.

Second, we measure whether a firm's R&D activities are organized in a centralized or decentralized manner. We define a firm's R&D organization structure as centralized if R&D activities are highly independent of business units and as decentralized if R&D activities are directly controlled by separate business units. The literature indicates that there is a trade-off between centralized and decentralized R&D structures (Azoulay and Lerner 2012). The advantage of adopting a decentralized R&D structure is that managers of R&D organizations (such as a pharmaceuticals development division) are likely to have superior knowledge about the local market and the need of customers and be better placed to prevent R&D employees from losing sight of market imperatives. On the other hand, decentralized R&D may prevent the pooling of knowledge and spillovers from R&D activities within other units of the firm, and managers of specific business units may lack the knowledge and skills for R&D activities that are non-local and/or explorative in nature. Centralized R&D (such as in a central research laboratory) can potentially overcome these drawbacks by providing a place for nonlocal research activities and long-term and explorative projects but runs the risk of losing information about customer needs and choosing R&D projects for their scientific interest. This trade-off suggests that decentralized R&D structures are more suitable for incremental innovation, while centralized R&D structures are more conducive to radical innovation. A number of studies report empirical findings providing evidence for this trade-off. For instance, Argyres and Silverman (2004) find that firms with centralized R&D structures generate innovations that have a higher level of impact than firms with decentralized R&D structures.[2] Using a sample of 71 large U.S. corporations taken from a survey of R&D executives, they construct measures of R&D organization structures and find a positive association between the degree of centralization and the number of patent citations received, which is a conventional proxy for the impact of innovations. Their finding suggests that centralized R&D structures are more likely to generate radical innovations than decentralized structures. In this study, we construct a centralization measure of R&D structures that is similar to Argyres and Silverman's (2004) and examine its association with the degree to which innovations are radical or incremental in nature.[3,4]

1.2.2 Staged Project Management

The management and funding of R&D projects often proceeds in stages. For example, the "Stage-Gate" method proposed by Cooper (1988, 2017) sets concrete interim

---

[2] Also see Argyres et al. (2020), who find that the positive link between centralized R&D and the impact and depth of innovation works through the increase in the connectedness of internal inventor networks: researchers in centralized R&D structures are likely to undertake technological search of greater breath so as to produce more radical innovations that benefit multiple divisions within the firm.

[3] Argyres and Silverman (2004) and Argyres et al. (2020) use the share of the R&D budget that is allocated by corporate headquarters as another measure for the degree of centralization of R&D structures. Meanwhile, Arora et al. (2011, 2014) develop yet another empirical measure of the decentralization of R&D, namely, the share of patents assigned to affiliates (as opposed to the parent).

[4] Although we define the degree of decentralization/centralization of R&D structures in terms of the degree of independence from a firm's business units, it should be noted that R&D decentralization and the delegation of authority over R&D activities may be closely intertwined. In fact, some studies (e.g., Argyres and Silverman 2004; Acemoglu et al. 2007) define decentralization in terms of the degree of delegation. Using our survey, we examine the correlation between delegation and decentralization in footnote 19 in Sect. 1.5.3.

1.2 Key Questions and Related Literature

goals, referred to as "gates" or "milestones," in each stage of an R&D project, and the project is continued only if the milestones are met. It is also well known that venture capital (VC) investors typically make staged investments in venture firms, holding open the option of abandoning a venture firm if it fails to meet milestones (Sahlman 1990). The literature on VC finds that staging is a way for VC investors (principals) to monitor firms (agents) and mitigate agency problems (Gompers 1995; Kaplan and Strömberg 2003; Tian 2011) and that staging allows VC investors to learn about the agent over time and sort good projects from bad ones (Dahiya and Ray 2012). On the other hand, staging may lead to underinvestment by VC investors at the early stage (Wang and Zhou 2004) and exacerbate venture firms' focus on short-term success to continually look attractive to VC investors (Cornelli and Yosha 2003; Yung 2019).

In our view, the two-period model of the innovation process presented by Manso (2011) captures the advantages and disadvantages of staging well. In the model, the agent chooses between two actions in each stage: exploration or exploitation. Exploitation consists of well know actions or work methods to achieve incremental innovations with a known probability of success, while exploration consists of new untested actions or work methods to achieve radical innovations. The probability of success of radical innovations is unknown and the agent updates his/her beliefs about the probability of success once he/she has attempted radical innovation in the first stage. Because both actions entail private costs to the agent, the agent has an incentive to shirk. Manso's (2011) model makes two predictions with respect to staging. First, the effect that the threat of termination has on exploration is ambiguous because it prevents the agent from shirking but encourages the agent to choose a project with a higher probability of success, i.e., exploitation. Depending on which of these two effects is more important, staging of innovation projects may either encourage or discourage an agent from choosing exploration. Second, feedback on interim outcomes of the project provides incentives for exploration because it allows interim adjustments by the agent and increases the probability of success of the project. Several empirical studies examine Manso's (2011) predictions. Ederer and Manso (2013) provide experimental evidence on the effects of termination. Specifically, they conducted a laboratory experiment in which participants operate a hypothetical computerized lemonade stand and choose between exploitation, i.e., making minor adjustments to the business strategy (e.g., fine-tuning the product mix of lemonade), or exploration, i.e., making major adjustments to the business strategy (e.g., changing the location of the lemonade stand). To study the effect of termination, they divide participants into two groups: one whose lemonade stands were eliminated if they underperformed in the first half of the experiment and another whose lemonade stands continued regardless of the performance in the first half. Ederer and Manso (2013) find that participants in the latter group were more likely to choose an explorative strategy, suggesting that the threat of termination undermines the incentives for explorative innovation. Meanwhile, using a sample of VC-backed initial public offering (IPO) firms, Mao et al. (2014) find that IPO firms were less innovative, as measured by the number of patents granted and the number of future citations received by each patent, when VC investors held a larger number of VC financing rounds (stages). Further, in the realm of scientific research, Azoulay et al. (2011) examine whether the funding program of the Howard Hughes Medical Institute (HHMI), which tolerates early failure and provides detailed and high-quality feedback to the researcher, encourages exploration more than the funding program of the National Institutes of Health (NIH), which imposes more stringent interim reviews. They find that researchers who used HHMI grants produced higher-impact articles than NIH-funded researchers. The empirical results obtained by Azoulay et al. (2011) suggest that more "forgiving" scientific research grants with extensive feedback lead to more explorative innovations than grants with stricter interim reviews.

As explained above, staging is prevalent in the management and financing of R&D projects and VC investment in start-up firms, and there are several theoretical and empirical studies that examine the determinants and effects of staging in the context of such firms. However, as far as we are aware, there are few empirical studies that investigate staging in the context of R&D projects. An exception is the study by Andries and Hünermund (2020), which examines the impact of staging on the initiation/abandonment of innovation projects. Our survey contributes to the literature by providing a systematic description of the staging in R&D projects.

Concretely, we first ask respondent firms whether they implement staged project management of their R&D projects and examine the statistical association between staging and the likelihood of making product innovations as well as the association between staging and the choice between explorative and exploitative innovation. Since the VC literature surveyed above suggests that there are both advantages and disadvantages to staging, it is an empirical matter whether the correlation between staging and making product innovations is positive or negative and whether staging is correlated with exploration or exploitation.

In addition, we ask the following questions to examine whether our data are consistent with Manso's (2011) predictions with respect to staging. First, to examine the effect of the threat of termination on exploration, we ask whether a firm sets intermediate goals ("milestones") for the interim evaluation of a project. If the answer to this question is positive, we then ask to what extent the firm considers whether the milestones were achieved when assessing whether to terminate/suspend or continue the R&D project. Second, to examine the effect of feedback on exploration, we ask whether a firm provides feedback on the interim evaluation results to the R&D personnel in charge of an R&D project. If the answer to this question is positive, we then ask who provides feedback: other research teams in the R&D organizations within the firm, non-R&D business units within the firm and the head office, or external experts outside the firm. Using these two questions in our survey, we examine how the threat of termination and feedback is associated with the success of R&D projects and the choice between radical/incremental innovation.

1.2.3 Compensation and Incentive Schemes for R&D Personnel

Incentives play an in important role in the organization of R&D activities. A key issue therefore is how firms assess and compensate/reward their R&D personnel. Since the interests of employees and their employers are not always aligned, many studies have examined how firms design compensation contracts and provide incentives to induce employees to work in the firm's interest (see Prendergast (1999) for a survey). However, these studies also highlight that providing incentives for innovation is especially difficult. Because innovative projects are risky and their outcomes are unpredictable, standard pay-for-performance compensation is less effective in inducing effort in the case of R&D than other employees. Worse still, pay-for-performance compensation may be detrimental in getting R&D personnel and/or managers to choose explorative R&D projects because they are, by definition, more likely to fail (Holmström 1989; Manso 2011).[5] To deal with such problems, Manso (2011) argues, tolerance for early failure and reward for long-term success is essential for motivating radical innovation. However, while Manso lists several long-term compensations plans for executives and managers (e.g., stock options with long vesting period), he does not discuss long-term incentive schemes for employees. Although providing incentive schemes for R&D employees is fraught with difficulties, previous studies—which we outline below—as well as pre-interviews we conducted with managers of R&D organizations and human resources departments in Japanese firms suggest that many firms try to devise compensation and incentive schemes for R&D personnel to motivate innovation. In our survey, we focus on the following aspects of human resource management practices for R&D personnel to understand what Japanese firms do.

First, we ask about the relative weights given to ability and performance in R&D employee evaluations, where ability refers to the ability demonstrated in performing a job and performance refers to the level of achievement in performing the job. Standard agency theory predicts that a firm will not adopt pay-for-performance when performance measures are noisy in the sense that they do not adequately reflect employees' input of effort (Holmström and Milgrom 1991). Because more ambitious projects entail larger risk and uncertainty, theory suggests that firms are less likely to employ performance evaluation in the case of explorative R&D projects. However, there is little empirical support for a negative relationship between the risk (uncertainty) of projects and the use of pay-for-performance (Prendergast 2011). To explain why this is the case, Prendergast (2002) constructs a theoretical model that predicts that uncertainty may be positively related to pay-for-performance through a different mechanism. Specifically, he argues that uncertain environments lead to the delegation of responsibility to employees because in very uncertain settings, it is hard

---

[5] Because incentives, including pay-for-performance, may not be effective in inducing innovation, some studies postulate contractual incompleteness, based on the recognition that writing incentive contracts is too complex and costly. See, for example, Aghion and Tirole (1994) and Hellman and Thiele (2011).

to tell employees what to do. Because the principal delegates control to employees, performance-based pay becomes the only way to compensate for employees' unobservable effort. Consistent with Prendergast's (2002) prediction, Foss and Laursen (2005) find that the extent to which firms innovate is positively correlated with the use of pay-for-performance. Using our survey, we examine whether there is a link between the use of performance evaluation on the one hand and the likelihood of product innovations and of explorative/exploitative innovations on the other.

Second, to further hone in on human resource management practices in more detail, we ask firms whether they employ various practices for the evaluation of R&D personnel from a list we provide in our questionnaire. Some of the items on the list refer to R&D employees' performance (e.g., patent applications/registrations), while others refer to their ability (e.g., the acquisition of qualifications/degrees). Using the responses, we examine the link between performance-based and ability-based evaluation on the one hand and innovation outcomes on the other from a slightly different perspective than the previous question.

Third, we ask firms about pecuniary and non-pecuniary incentive schemes for R&D personnel. Pecuniary incentives are monetary rewards based on the outcomes of innovative activities by R&D personnel (e.g., rewards based on the number of patent applications), while non-pecuniary incentives are non-monetary rewards/subsidies (e.g., dispatch to university and/or support for studying abroad), which may increase R&D employees' intrinsic motivation for innovation. Several studies suggest that pecuniary incentives that provide extrinsic motivation for workers may adversely affect their intrinsic motivation, such as pride in their work and enjoyment in carrying out tasks (Bénabou and Tirole 2003; Kreps 1997). In the context of R&D management, such intrinsic motivation includes, for instance, the intellectual challenge of contributing to scientific and technological progress. Previous empirical studies that examine the link between pecuniary and non-pecuniary incentives and innovation outputs report mixed results. Using firm-level panel data for listed firms in Japan, Onishi (2013) reports a positive association between monetary compensation plans for employee inventions and the number of patent citations but no association with the number of patent applications. In contrast, using a 2001 court decision that effectively forced Japanese firms to strengthen pecuniary incentives based on the commercial success of an invention as an exogenous instrument for pecuniary incentives, Onishi et al. (2021) find that pecuniary incentives decreased the number of science-based patents. Using individual-level data for R&D employees, Sauermann and Cohen (2010) examine the relationship between extrinsic and intrinsic motives of R&D personnel on the one hand and their innovative performance on the other hand. They find that R&D employees with stronger motives such as pay (extrinsic motive) and intellectual challenge and independence (intrinsic motives) produce a larger number of patent applications (innovative outputs). Sauermann and Cohen's findings (2010) suggest that both extrinsic and intrinsic motives are important for innovation.[6] Our study differs from Sauermann and Cohen's (2010) in that we ask firms about the pecuniary and non-pecuniary incentive schemes they employ, while Sauermann and Cohen (2010) ask employees about their subjective motives.

Finally, we use some of the questions outlined above to examine whether reward for long-term success (Manso 2011) is correlated with innovation. Specifically, the question about the evaluation of R&D personnel contains as one of the possible criteria the "amount of sales generated by new products to which the R&D employee contributed," while the question about incentive schemes for R&D personnel contains as one of the possible incentives "rewards based on the amount of profits from inventions and patents (invention reward schemes)." In addition, we regard promotion as another potential reward for long-term success. The questionnaire contains a question asking whether any of the directors on the board of the firm belonged to an R&D organization within the firm in the past, and we regard the answer to this question as an indicator of whether promotion to the board is possible and hence a potential incentive for R&D personnel. Promotion is one of the most common means of rewarding white-collar workers for effort and long-term outcomes, and a substantial share of directors on the boards of Japanese firms are promoted internally. However, to what level in the hierarchy R&D personnel can be promoted may vary across firms. We use this question to examine whether the possibility of promotion to top-level management works as an effective incentive scheme for innovation.

1.2.4 Risk Preferences and Corporate Culture

Some studies suggest that corporate culture, which is defined as "a set of norms and values that are widely shared and strongly held throughout the organization" (O'Reilly and Chatman 1996), may be an important driver of firm performance. The empirical study by Guiso et al. (2015) shows that corporate culture impacts a firm's performance more than corporate governance. Manso (2011) argues that nurturing a corporate culture that encourages experimentation and tolerates early failure is important for innovation because it is difficult, if not impossible, to devise compensation and incentive schemes that credibly motivate innovation among employees, as discussed in Sect. 1.2.2. Some studies find empirical evidence that is consistent with Manso's (2011) argument. For instance, Ederer and Manso (2013) show that risk aversion plays an important role in explaining differences in participants' behavior in their hypothetical lemonade stand experiment (see Sect. 1.2.2). Meanwhile, using data on large pharmaceutical firms' drug development decisions, Krieger et al. (2022) show that risk aversion leads firms to underinvest in radical innovation. Further, in experiments with master's degree students, Carson et al. (2020) find that participants that are more tolerant of risk are more likely to choose higher-risk projects. In

---

[6] Dewett (2007) reports that the intrinsic motivation of R&D employees is positively associated with their willingness to take risk, but that the statistical association between intrinsic motivation and employee creativity depends on the proxy used for creativity.

contrast, financial rewards that encourage participants to disproportionately undertake higher-risk projects do not induce most participants to invest in such projects. In the realm of the venture capital (VC) industry, Tian and Wang (2014) report that IPO firms backed by more failure-tolerant VC investors are more innovative. Finally, based on a survey of large North American firms, Graham et al. (2021) report that 57% of senior executives surveyed think that corporate culture has a "big effect" on their firms' creativity while 41% think that corporate culture has a "big effect" on their firms' willingness to take on risky projects. Constructing measures of cultural values from their survey, Graham et al. (2021) find that "adaptability" is positively correlated with creativity while "results-orientation" is negatively correlated with creativity.

In our survey, we ask several questions to measure a firm's risk preferences and corporate culture and examine their impact on innovation. To measure a firm's risk preferences, we included the following three questions in our survey. First, we asked firms whether they were taking appropriate risks in their R&D projects. Asking a similar question in their survey, Graham et al. (2021) report that 60% of respondent firms felt they took the "right amount of risk," while 29% said they took "too little risk" and 11% said they took "too much risk." Second, we set a hypothetical question about an R&D project which was expected to generate gross sales of 100 million yen if it was successful but gross sales of 0 yen if it failed and asked about the maximum amount that respondent firms would be willing to invest in this project (i.e., their reservation price). It was assumed that the probability of success was 10% and the expected payoff of the project accordingly was 10 million yen. In our analysis below, we classify respondent firms that were willing to invest 10 million yen as "risk-neutral," those willing to invest less than 10 million yen as "risk-averse," and those willing to invest more than 10 million yen as "risk-tolerant." Using a similar survey question about a hypothetical lottery ticket, Cramer et al. (2002) construct a measure of risk aversion to examine whether risk aversion affects individuals' choice of becoming an entrepreneur. Third, we measure firms' risk preferences by asking them to choose between two otherwise identical projects. Project 1 has a greater net present value (NPV) but negative cash flow for the first few years, whereas Project 2 has positive cash flow throughout its duration but has a smaller NPV. Graham et al. (2021) ask a similar question in their survey and report that, somewhat surprisingly, 41% of firms chose the NPV-inferior project (which would be Project 2 in our case). They also show that about 80% of firms that chose the NPV-superior project (corresponding to Project 1 in our case) say that corporate culture plays a role in their preference for the NPV-superior project.

To measure firms' corporate culture, we employ the Competing Values Framework (CVF) proposed by Cameron et al. (2014), who argue that the CVF provides a way to characterize organizational culture in simple terms. Specifically, the framework consists of two dimensions that express the tensions ("competing values") in organizations, which result in four categories (quadrants): *Collaborate (Clan)*, *Control (Hierarchy)*, *Compete (Market)*, and *Create (Adhocracy)*.

Figure 1.1 provides a schematic representation. One dimension focuses on the orientation toward internal maintenance versus external positioning, while the other

1.2 Key Questions and Related Literature

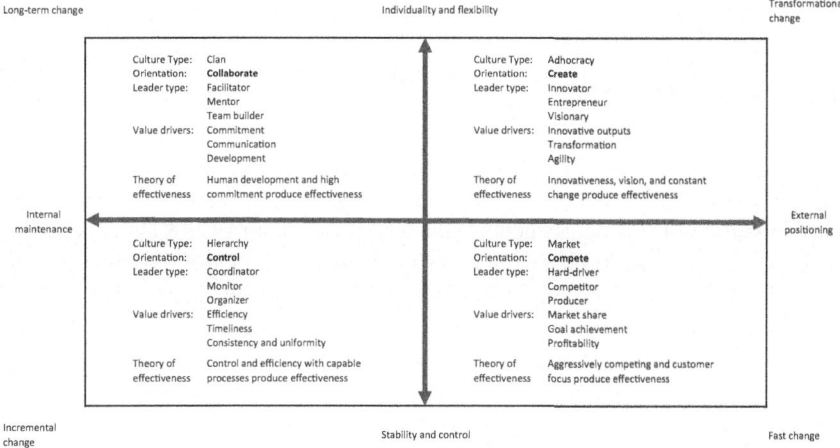

Fig. 1.1 The competing values framework (*Source* Cameron et al. 2014, Fig. 3.1)

dimension focuses on the orientation toward individuality and flexibility on the one hand versus stability and control on the other. Turning to the quadrants, firms with a *collaborate*-oriented culture attempt to develop human competencies and cooperative processes by building consensus. In contrast, firms with a *control*-oriented culture attempt to improve internal organizational efficiency through control mechanisms. These are two internally oriented culture types that are differentiated in terms of the second dimension based on their individuality and flexibility (*collaborate*-orientation) or stability and control (*control*-orientation). Next, firms with a *compete*-oriented culture seek to enhance their competitiveness and prioritize customers and shareholders. As a result, firms with a *compete*-oriented culture tend to judge success in terms of their market share, revenue, and profitability. In contrast, firms with a *create*-oriented culture seek to create future opportunities in the marketplace through innovation and encourage entrepreneurship and changes. As a result, firms with a *create*-oriented culture tend to judge success in terms of the development of new products, services and technologies. These are two externally oriented culture types, differentiated again in terms of the second dimension based on their individuality and flexibility (*create*-orientation) or stability and control (*compete*-orientation). In our survey, we asked respondent firms to choose up to three words to describe their corporate culture from a total of eight words corresponding to the four quadrants. Fiordelisi and Ricci (2014) use the CVF to examine the effect of corporate culture on the relationship between firm performance and CEO turnover. However, as far as we are aware, there are no empirical studies that examine the effect of corporate culture on innovation using the CVF.

1.3 Methodology

1.3.1 Survey Design

Before designing the "Survey of R&D Management Practices," we visited five R&D organizations on-site to meet with the managers and directors of R&D organizations and/or human resources departments and asked about the firms' R&D management practices. We then incorporated their insights, as well as those from the related literature described in Sect. 1.2, in the first draft of the survey questionnaire. Next, we circulated the initial draft among them and asked for comments. In addition, we asked three other R&D employees at different firms to answer the draft survey questionnaire and provide feedback. Based on the comments and feedback, we then made numerous changes to the questionnaire.

We focus on R&D management practices among business enterprises with systematic R&D operations. Specifically, we target business enterprises with paid-in capital of 100 million yen or more that undertake R&D activities. Because many firms in service industries do not conduct R&D, we target firms in manufacturing (Japan Standard Industrial Classification [JSIC]: 09–32), information and communications (JSIC: 37–41), and wholesale and retail trade (JSIC: 50–55). We construct our sample by identifying firms in the 2017 and 2018 rounds of the Survey of Research and Development conducted by the Statistics Bureau of Japan, Ministry of Internal Affairs and Communications meeting these criteria.[7] There were 3,456 such firms. It should be noted that since we do not include firms with paid-in capital of less than 100 million yen and firms in industries other than manufacturing, information and communications, and wholesale and retail trade, our results may not reflect R&D management practices and innovation among Japanese firms overall.

We then conducted our "Survey of R&D Management Practices" in January–February 2020." Survey questionnaires were sent out to the 3,456 firms and we asked for questions to be answered by the person(s) most qualified to respond with regard to the following: (1) R&D expenditure, R&D personnel, and R&D organizational structure, (2) R&D project management, (3) personnel evaluation of researchers and engineers, and (4) R&D outputs. In addition to these questions, we asked firms to provide some details on the person who responded to our questionnaire (such as the job title and number of years with the company). Many respondents were in managerial positions of R&D organizations or general affairs divisions and had worked for their company for "more than 20 years." The survey consists of up to 32 questions (depending on the survey path taken), and we checked that it took about 25–35 min to complete all questions. We asked respondents to provide answers as of fiscal year (FY) 2018 and on a non-consolidated basis, unless stated otherwise. The survey questionnaire that we sent to respondent firms and a glossary of terms attached to the survey for respondents' reference are provided in the Appendix.

---

[7] For details of the Survey of Research and Development, see the following website: https://www.stat.go.jp/english/data/kagaku/index.html (accessed 16 November 2021).

The filled-in surveys were returned by mail or via a website by the end of March 2020. To increase the survey response rate, we sent reminder emails and/or made reminder telephone calls to firms that had not responded to the questionnaire. We also checked the accuracy of the answers to the questions by examining whether they were mutually and/or logically consistent and asked respondents for confirmation when necessary. Following this procedure, we were left with 611 valid responses for a response rate of 17.7%. Of these 611 responses, 150 (24.5%) were received by mail and 461 (75.5%) online. We summarize the results of the survey in Ono et al. (2020) and in September 2020 sent this summary to firms that had responded to the questionnaire.

1.3.2 Summary Statistics

This subsection provides summary statistics of the sample that we use in the subsequent analyses. In constructing the sample, we match our survey data with data taken from the Survey of Research and Development. Specifically, we use the 2019 Survey of Research and Development, which reports the basic characteristics of the firms as of FY 2018.[8] We use the Survey of Research and Development for several important variables that characterize respondent firms, such as their sales turnover and R&D expenditure as well as the total number of employees, number of R&D employees, and employees with a doctorate degree—information that is not included in the survey.

Table 1.1 presents the number of firms in the sample overall by industry and firm size. The latter is measured in terms of the number of employees. We classify the sample into small firms (with 300 or fewer employees), medium-sized firms (with 301 to 1,000 employees), and large firms (with more than 1,000 employees). Small firms make up the largest share of the sample (51.4%), followed by medium-sized firms (31.9%), and large firms (16.7%). In terms of industry, the sample consists of 558 manufacturing firms (91.3%) and 53 non-manufacturing firms (8.7%). Table 1.1 breaks down manufacturing into five subcategories and non-manufacturing into two subcategories. Within manufacturing, the top two industries in terms of the number of observations are the machinery and equipment industry with 226 firms (37.0%) and the chemical, petroleum, coal, and plastic products industry with 161 firms (26.4%). The former includes manufacturers of motor vehicles, parts and accessories, while the latter includes manufacturers of pharmaceuticals and medicinal chemicals, two industries that spend a large amount on R&D.

The firm size distribution varies across industries. The share of small firms is larger in non-manufacturing (73.6%) than that in manufacturing (49.3%). Within manufacturing, small firms account for the largest share in the chemical, petroleum,

---

[8] There are several firms for which data from the 2019 Survey of Research and Development were unavailable. We use data from either the 2018 or 2017 Survey of Research and Development for these firms.

Table 1.1 Number of firms in the sample

| | Entire sample | | By firm size: | | | | | |
| | | | Small | | Medium | | Large | |
	N	Share (%)	N	Share (%)	N	Share (%)	N	Share (%)
Entire sample	611	(100.0)	314	[51.4]	195	[31.9]	102	[16.7]
By industry								
Manufacturing industries	558	(91.3)	275	[49.3]	186	[33.3]	97	[17.4]
Food, beverages, and tobacco	60	(9.8)	28	[46.7]	22	[36.7]	10	[16.7]
Chemical, petroleum, coal, and plastic products	161	(26.4)	94	[58.4]	47	[29.2]	20	[12.4]
Iron, steel, and non-ferrous metals products	56	(9.2)	23	[41.1]	23	[41.1]	10	[17.9]
Machinery and equipment	226	(37.0)	103	[45.6]	76	[33.6]	47	[20.8]
Miscellaneous manufacturing	55	(9.0)	27	[49.1]	18	[32.7]	10	[18.2]
Non-manufacturing industries	53	(8.7)	39	[73.6]	9	[17.0]	5	[9.4]
Information and communications	31	(5.1)	21	[67.7]	5	[16.1]	5	[16.1]
Wholesale and retail trade	22	(3.6)	18	[81.8]	4	[18.2]	0	[0.0]

Note Figures in parentheses () represent the percentage share of firms in each industry in the total number of firms, whereas figures in square brackets [] represent the percentage share of firms of a particular size in the total number of firms in that industry

1.3 Methodology

Table 1.2 Number of employees

	N	Mean	Median	S.D.
Entire sample	611	764.6	287.0	1,658.0
By industry				
Manufacturing industries	558	792.4	310.5	1,704.5
Food, beverages, and tobacco	60	673.7	334.5	929.9
Chemical, petroleum, coal, and plastic products	161	514.1	238.0	735.2
Iron, steel, and non-ferrous metals products	56	1,013.9	401.5	2,309.8
Machinery and equipment	226	1,012.4	335.0	2,236.5
Miscellaneous manufacturing	55	607.1	308.0	782.6
Non-manufacturing industries	53	471.4	122.0	1,014.5
Information and communications	31	678.0	103.0	1,289.5
Wholesale and retail trade	22	180.3	167.0	146.6

coal, and plastic products industries (58.4%). In contrast, large firms account for the largest share in the machinery and equipment industry (20.8%).

Table 1.2 provides descriptive statistics on the number of employees by industry. The overall sample mean is 765 employees, while the median is 287 for the whole sample, suggesting that the distribution of the number of employees is highly skewed. This is because the sample includes nine firms that have more than 5,000 employees. Firms in manufacturing industries have a larger number of employees than those in non-manufacturing industries. In particular, firms in the iron, steel, and non-ferrous metal products industry (mean: 1,014) and the machinery and equipment industry (mean: 1,012) have a larger number of employees than their counterparts in other industries.

1.4 R&D Outcomes and Inputs

1.4.1 R&D Outcomes

In the survey, we define the success of R&D outcomes in terms of whether a firm developed process innovations or product innovations during the past three years, from FY2016 to FY2018.[9] Table 1.3 provides an overview of the share of firms that

---

[9] We define "process innovation" as new or significantly improved production processes and methods of providing services and/or delivering products or support activities that include significant improvements in techniques, equipment, and/or software. We define "product innovation" as new or significantly improved goods or services with respect to their technical specifications, components and materials, software in the product, user friendliness, or other functional characteristics that include new combinations of existing technologies or technology upgrades of existing goods or services. For details, see the glossary of terms in the Appendix. The definitions of process

Table 1.3 Firms that introduced process and product innovations

	N	Process innovation		Product innovation	
		Share (%)	S.D.	Share (%)	S.D.
Entire sample	609	44.5	49.7	54.4	49.9
By firm size					
(a) Small	313	36.4	48.2	47.0	50.0
(b) Medium	194	44.9	49.9	56.7	49.7
(c) Large	102	68.6	46.6	72.5	44.8
By industry					
Manufacturing industries	558	46.8	49.9	55.0	49.8
Food, beverages, and tobacco	60	51.7	50.4	71.7	45.4
Chemical, petroleum, and plastic products	161	44.1	49.8	49.7	50.2
Iron, steel, and non-ferrous metals products	56	42.9	49.9	55.4	50.2
Machinery and equipment	226	46.0	50.0	52.7	50.0
Miscellaneous manufacturing	55	56.4	50.1	61.8	49.0
Non-manufacturing industries	51	19.6	40.1	47.1	50.4
Information and communications	30	20.0	40.7	46.7	50.7
Wholesale and retail trade	21	19.0	40.2	47.6	51.2
Difference	N	Share (%)	S.E.	Share (%)	S.E.
(a)–(b), Small vs. Medium	507	−8.4*	4.5	−9.7**	4.6
(b)–(c), Medium vs. Large	296	−23.8***	6.0	−15.8***	5.9
(a)–(c), Small vs. Large	415	−32.2***	5.5	−25.6***	5.6

Note ***, **, and * indicate significance at the 1, 5, and 10% levels respectively

introduced process and product innovations by firm size and industry. This and all following tables report the mean and the standard deviation of the variables and test differences between subsamples using a two-sample equal variance *t*-test.[10] Among firm size categories, we choose two out of three categories and test the difference between the two subsample means. *, **, and *** in tables denote statistical significance at the 10%, 5%, and 1% levels, respectively. For some highly skewed variables, we also report the median.

---

and product innovation and the novelty of product innovation (Table 1.4) are based on the Oslo Manual 2018 by the Organisation for Economic Co-operation and Development, which provides international guidelines on innovation statistics.

[10] We use *t*-tests for all variables and do not use binomial tests for categorical variables. As robustness checks, we conducted binomial tests for several categorical variables and confirmed that there is no substantial difference between the *t*-tests and the binomial tests for our sample sizes.

1.4 R&D Outcomes and Inputs

Table 1.4 Product innovation by novelty of products

	N	New-to-market products only		New-to-firm products only		Both types of products	
		Share (%)	S.D.	Share (%)	S.D.	Share (%)	S.D.
Entire sample	329	17.3	37.9	41.3	49.3	41.3	49.3
By firm size							
(a) Small	147	25.2	43.5	36.1	48.2	38.8	48.9
(b) Medium	110	10.9	31.3	48.2	50.2	40.9	49.4
(c) Large	72	11.1	31.6	41.7	49.6	47.2	50.3
By industry							
Manufacturing industries	305	17.4	38.0	41.0	49.3	41.6	49.4
Food, beverages, and tobacco	43	23.3	42.7	44.2	50.2	32.6	47.4
Chemical, petroleum, and plastic products	80	13.8	34.7	38.8	49.0	47.5	50.3
Iron, steel, and non-ferrous metals products	31	12.9	34.1	48.4	50.8	38.7	49.5
Machinery and equipment	118	18.6	39.1	39.0	49.0	42.4	49.6
Miscellaneous manufacturing	33	18.2	39.2	42.4	50.2	39.4	49.6
Non-manufacturing industries	24	16.7	38.1	45.8	50.9	37.5	49.5
Information and communications	14	21.4	42.6	35.7	49.7	42.9	51.4
Wholesale and retail trade	10	10.0	31.6	60.0	51.6	30.0	48.3
Difference	N	Share (%)	S.E.	Share (%)	S.E.	Share (%)	S.E.
(a)–(b), Small vs. Medium	257	14.26***	4.89	−12.13*	6.18	−2.13	6.19
(b)–(c), Medium vs. Large	182	−0.20	4.77	6.52	7.58	−6.31	7.54
(a)–(c), Small vs. Large	219	14.06**	5.76	−5.61	7.00	−8.45	7.10

Note ***, **, and * indicate significance at the 1, 5, and 10% levels respectively

Table 1.3 shows that the percentage shares of firms that developed process innovations and product innovations are 44.5% and 54.4%, respectively. Larger firms are more likely to develop both process and product innovations. By industry, firms in the information and communications industry show the lowest propensity to produce process innovations (20.0%) and product innovations (46.7%), while those in the food, beverage, and tobacco industry show the highest propensity to produce product innovations (71.7%).

For firms that introduced product innovations in the market, the survey asked follow-up questions on the novelty of the products, and we define two types of product novelty. The first refers to new or significantly improved goods or services that no competitors were offering (referred to as "new-to-market" products), while the second refers to new or improved goods or services that were the same as or very similar to ones already offered by competitors (referred to as "new-to-firm" products).

Table 1.4 reports the percentage shares of firms that introduced new-to-market and/or new-to-firm products during FY 2016–2018. Of the 329 product innovators, 17.3% (57 firms) developed new-to-market products but did not develop new-to-firm products ("new-to-market products only"). Meanwhile, 41.3% of product innovators (136 firms) developed new-to-firm products but did not develop new-to-market products ("new-to-firm products only"), and 41.3% (136 firms) developed both types of products ("both types of products").

The percentage shares of "new-to-market products only," "new-to-firm products only," and "both types of products" firms are similar for medium-sized and large firms. By contrast, a considerably larger share of small firms (25.2%) than large and medium-sized firms (ca. 11%) generate new-to-market product innovations. On the other hand, the share of small firms generating new-to-firm product innovations (36.1%) is lower than that of medium-sized firms (48.2%) and large firms (41.7%). These results suggest that small firms are more oriented toward developing new-to-market products. This may be because small firms have a comparative disadvantage in accumulating intangible assets such as reputation and brand recognition and therefore seek to build an advantage through the introduction of novel products. In contrast, large firms tend to pursue both types of product innovation: the percentage share of "both types of products" for large firms is 47.2%, which is higher than that for small firm (38.8%) and medium-sized firms (40.9%). It should be noted, however, that the differences among the three types of firms are not statistically significant.

The distribution of firms in terms of the type of product innovation also varies across industries. The food, beverage, and tobacco industry has the highest share of firms generating new-to-market products only (23.3%), while the wholesale and retail trade industry has the highest share of firms generating new-to-firm products only (60.0%), and the chemical, petroleum, coal, and plastic products industry has the highest share of firms generating both types of product innovation (47.5%).

In the tables below we report summary statics for the responses to our survey questions by firm size, by whether a firm has made product innovations ("innovator" or "non-innovator"), and in terms of the novelty of product innovations that a firm has made ("new-to-market" or "new-to-firm"). Because we focus on the interaction between R&D management practices and innovation, we examine whether the summary statistics for various R&D management practices differ between product innovators and non-innovators by conducting two-sample equal variance t-tests.[11] We recognize that differences between product innovators and non-innovators may reflect differences in firm characteristics such as firm size. While it is beyond the scope of this study to examine this possibility in detail, we add footnotes where we suspect that correlations may be spurious.

Because our sample consists of firms with systematic R&D operations, it is likely that non-innovators, at least some of them, have tried to create product innovations but failed in the past three years. In the analysis below, we therefore assume that non-innovators have attempted to make product innovations but failed to do so. In addition, we use the novelty of product innovations among product innovators to examine the tension between explorative and exploitative innovation. For this purpose, we assume that firms that introduced new-to-market products in the preceding three years pursued explorative R&D, whereas those that introduced new-to-firm products in the preceding three years pursued exploitative R&D. More specifically, in the analysis below, we regard firms that introduced "new-to-market products only" as firms creating explorative innovations and firms that introduced "new-to-firm products only" as firms creating exploitative innovations.[12] Based on these assumptions with regard to product non-innovators and product novelty, we examine whether the results of the survey are consistent with the predictions of the related literature we outlined in Sect. 1.2.

1.4.2 R&D Inputs: R&D Expenditures

This subsection reviews respondent firms' total R&D expenditure in FY 2018, their funding sources for R&D expenditure, and the importance of various factors taken into account when determining the level of R&D expenditure.[13]

1.4.2.1 Amount of R&D Expenditure

Table 1.5 reports summary statistics on firms' total amount of R&D expenditure and its ratio to total sales (referred to as the R&D-to-sales ratio). The mean of R&D

---

[11] We do not report summary statistics for process innovations in the tables below because in many cases the results are qualitatively similar to those for product innovations. Because we also focus on product novelty, we chose to report the results for product innovation.

[12] Firms that developed "both types of products" are likely to pursue both explorative and exploitative R&D. We do not report summary statistics for these firms because we cannot examine whether R&D management practices differ between firms that pursue explorative R&D and firms that pursue exploitative R&D when we use this subsample.

[13] "R&D expenditure" in the survey refers to the total amount of expenses on R&D, irrespective of whether such expenses are funded internally (e.g., through retained earnings) or externally (e.g., through grants from the government). R&D expenditure includes expenditures spent both within and outside respondent firms.

Table 1.5 R&D expenditure

	R&D expenditure (million yen)				R&D-to-sales ratio (%)			
	N	Mean	S.D.	Median	N	Mean	S.D.	Median
Entire sample	611	1,669.8	7,446.8	186.1	610	4.3	13.2	1.8
By firm size								
(a) Small	314	159.7	280.6	74.6	313	5.2	16.9	1.8
(b) Medium	195	640.5	845.4	335.1	195	2.9	6.3	1.6
(c) Large	102	8,285.9	16,732.2	1,930.1	102	4.3	9.6	1.7
Non-innovators vs. Innovators								
(d) Non-innovators	278	687.0	2,319.6	129.8	277	3.9	9.1	1.5
(e) Innovators	331	2,501.3	9,822.1	218.9	331	4.3	14.7	1.9
New-to-market vs. New-to-firm innovators								
(e1) New-to-market (NTM) innovators	57	661.3	2,255.3	156.4	57	9.4	31.8	1.3
(e2) New-to-firm (NTF) innovators	136	1,976.0	6,072.7	203.5	136	3.0	5.6	1.8
Difference	N	Mean	S.E.		N	Mean	S.E.	
(a)–(b), Small vs. Medium	509	−480.8***	51.7		508	2.3*	1.3	
(b)–(c), Medium vs. Large	297	−7,645.3***	1,199.3		297	−1.4	0.9	
(a)–(c), Small vs. Large	416	−8,126.1***	942.3		415	0.9	1.8	
(d)–(e), Non-innovators vs. Innovators	609	−1,814.3***	602.8		608	−0.5	1.0	
(e1)–(e2), NTM vs. NTF innovators	193	−1,314.7	828.3		193	6.4**	2.8	

Notes The R&D-to-sales ratio is defined as the ratio of firms' total R&D expenditure to total sales. ***, **, and * indicate significance at the 1, 5, and 10% levels respectively

1.4 R&D Outcomes and Inputs

expenditure for the entire sample is 1.67 billion yen, while the median is 186 million yen, suggesting that the distribution of R&D expenditure is highly skewed. Looking at the means for small, medium-sized, and large firms, we find, unsurprisingly, that larger firms spend a larger amount on R&D than small and medium-sized firm. We therefore also calculate the R&D-to-sales ratio to adjust for firm size and find that the mean of the R&D-to-sales ratio is 4.3%, while the median for the entire sample is 1.8%. Interestingly, we find that the mean of the R&D-to-sales ratio is highest for small firms (5.2%) and lowest for medium-sized firms (2.9%).

Innovating firms invest more in R&D than non-innovating firms. The mean of the R&D expenditure of innovating firms (2.50 billion yen) is 3.6 times larger than that of non-innovating firms (0.69 billion yen). However, the difference in the R&D-to-sales ratio between innovating firms (4.3%) and non-innovating firms (3.9%) turns out to be much smaller (1.1 times) and is statistically insignificant. This suggests that the difference in R&D expenditure may simply reflect the fact that large firms are more likely to succeed in making product innovations, as reported in Table 1.3. More importantly, the insignificant difference in the R&D-to-sales ratio between innovating firms and non-innovating firms suggests that factors other than R&D inputs, such as R&D management practices, which we will examine later, may be an important determinant of success in product innovation.

The total amount of R&D expenditure of new-to-market innovators (0.66 billion yen) is two-fifth as large as that of new-to-firm innovators (1.98 billion yen), but the difference between these subsamples is insignificant. By contrast, the R&D-to-sales ratio for new-to-market innovators (9.4%) is 3.1 times higher than that for new-to-firm innovators (3.0%) and the difference is statistically significant. This result indicates that once we control for the effect of firm size on R&D expenditure, new-to-market innovators invest more in their R&D activities than new-to-firm innovators.

1.4.2.2 Funding Sources for R&D Expenditure

The survey asked about the shares of different funding sources for R&D expenditure. Funding sources are classified into four categories. The first is funding from headquarters or the business unit to which the R&D organization belongs. The second is commissions received from other business units within the firm. The third is funding from outside the firm including commissions, subsidies, grants, etc. The fourth is sources other than these three categories.

Table 1.6 shows that 89.2% of R&D expenditure is provided by headquarters or the business unit to which an R&D organization belongs. The tendency for funding to come primarily from headquarters or the business unit to which the R&D organization belongs is particularly pronounced among small and medium-sized firms. On the other hand, among large firms, the sources of funding are more dispersed, with headquarters accounting for 84.6%, other business units for 8.0%, sources outside the firm for 5.2%, and other sources for 2.2%.

The differences in funding sources between non-innovators and innovators and between new-to-market innovators and new-to-firm innovators are small. One notable

Table 1.6 Funding sources for R&D expenditure

	N	Headquarters or the business unit to which the R&D organization belongs		Other business units within the firm		Outside the firm		Other	
		Mean (Share, %)	S.D.	Mean (Share, %)	S.D.	Mean (Share, %)	S.D.	Mean (Share, %)	S.D.
Entire sample	608	89.2	25.3	5.1	18.6	4.3	14.3	1.4	11.3
By firm size									
(a) Small	313	89.6	26.2	4.0	17.9	4.8	16.4	1.6	12.3
(b) Medium	195	90.8	22.9	5.2	18.9	3.1	10.4	0.8	7.1
(c) Large	100	84.6	26.5	8.0	19.9	5.2	13.8	2.2	14.1
Non-innovators vs. Innovators									
(d) Non-innovators	277	88.8	26.0	6.0	20.6	3.9	13.3	1.3	11.2
(e) Innovators	329	90.1	23.7	4.0	15.9	4.4	14.2	1.5	11.4
New-to-market vs. New-to-firm innovators									
(e1) New-to-market (NTM) innovators	57	87.3	28.6	1.8	13.3	5.6	15.3	5.3	21.8
(e2) New-to-firm (NTF) innovators	135	90.1	23.4	5.8	19.8	4.2	13.3	0.0	0.0
Difference	N	Mean (Share, %)	S.E.	Mean (Share, %)	S.E.	Mean (Share, %)	S.E.	Mean (Share, %)	S.E.
(a)–(b), Small vs. Medium	508	−1.22	2.28	−1.22	1.67	1.64	1.31	0.80	0.97
(b)–(c), Medium vs. Large	295	6.22**	2.98	−2.80	2.37	−2.01	1.43	−1.40	1.24
(a)–(c), Small vs. Large	413	4.99*	3.02	−4.02*	2.11	−0.37	1.82	−0.60	1.47
(d)–(e), Non-innovators vs. Innovators	606	−1.32	2.02	2.03	1.48	−0.55	1.12	−0.17	0.92
(e1)–(e2), NTM vs. NTF innovators	192	−2.81	3.96	−3.92	2.87	1.47	2.20	5.26***	1.87

Note ***, **, and * indicate significance at the 1, 5, and 10% levels respectively

feature is that new-to-market innovators obtain a higher share of funding from "other" sources (5.3%) than new-to-firm innovators (0.0%). However, the primary funding source for new-to-market innovators nevertheless also is the headquarters or the business unit to which the R&D organization belongs (87.3%).

1.4.2.3 Determinants of R&D Expenditure

Table 1.7 reports the importance of different factors that firms take into account when determining their total R&D expenditure. The survey provides six factors as possible determinants: gross sales in the previous year, profits in the previous year, R&D expenditure in the previous year, labor costs of the firm's R&D organization(s), cumulative costs of individual R&D projects, and annual sales goals for new products as a share of total sales. Firms were asked to answer whether each of these factors was "fully taken into account," "to some extent taken into account," "not very much taken into account," or "not taken into account at all." Table 1.7 reports the share of firms that took each of the factors either "fully" or "to some extent" into account. We assume that these factors are linked with the flexibility of the R&D budget. For example, if a firm puts more weight on gross sales or profits, the firm can flexibly adjust its R&D budget to its financial situation. By contrast, if a firm puts more weight on the R&D expenditure in the previous year and the cost of labor and research projects, the firm is likely to be bound by cost-related factors, making the research budget less flexible. In addition, based on anecdotal evidence that innovation-oriented firms set annual sales targets for new products as a share of total sales, the survey asked about the importance of this factor in determining the R&D budget.

The top three factors that the majority of firms in the sample said they took "fully" or "to some extent" into account are the R&D expenditure in the previous year (83.1%), the labor costs of their R&D organization(s) (67.8%), and profits in the previous year (67.4%). As for R&D expenditure in the previous year, 30.9% of firms "fully" take this into account as a determinant, and this share is much higher than those for the other factors. In contrast, the share of firms that "fully" or "to some extent" take into account annual sales goals for new products is only about 50%, making this the least important factor among the different options provided. To sum up, these results indicate that firms take several factors into account when determining their R&D budget, and cost-related factors are more important than performance-related factors. This tendency is more prominent among large firms. In fact, although the share of firms taking a particular factor into account is highest among large firms for all factors, the difference between large firms on the one hand and small and medium-sized ones on the other is significant only for cost-related factors, i.e., R&D expenditure, labor costs, and the cumulative costs of individual R&D projects.

Next, looking at differences between innovating and non-innovating firms shows that the former are more likely to take cost-related factors into account when deciding R&D expenditure. In addition, they are also more likely to consider performance-related factors in determining R&D expenditure. Specifically, 64.0% of innovating

Table 1.7 Determinants of total R&D expenditure

	N	Gross sales in the previous year		Profits in the previous year		R&D expenditure in the previous year		Labor costs of R&D organization(s)		Cumulative costs of individual R&D projects		Annual sales goals for new products as a share of total sales	
		Share (%)	S.D.	Share (%)	S.D.	Share (%)	S.D.	Share (%)	S.D.	Share (%)	S.D.	Share (%)	S.D.
Entire sample	611	58.8	49.3	67.4	46.9	83.1	37.5	67.8	46.8	64.3	47.9	50.7	50.0
By firm size													
(a) Small	314	56.4	49.7	65.9	47.5	76.4	42.5	62.7	48.4	62.7	48.4	51.0	50.1
(b) Medium	195	59.0	49.3	67.2	47.1	89.2	31.1	68.7	46.5	61.5	48.8	49.7	50.1
(c) Large	102	65.7	47.7	72.6	44.8	92.2	27.0	81.4	39.1	74.5	43.8	52.0	50.2
Non-innovators vs. Innovators													
(d) Non-innovators	278	52.2	50.0	61.2	48.8	78.4	41.2	62.9	48.4	61.2	48.8	47.5	50.0
(e) Innovators	331	64.0	48.1	72.5	44.7	87.0	33.7	71.6	45.2	66.8	47.2	53.2	50.0
New-to-market vs. New-to-firm innovators													
(e1) New-to-market (NTM) innovators	57	54.4	50.3	64.9	48.1	82.5	38.4	75.4	43.4	64.9	48.1	54.4	50.3
(e2) New-to-firm (NTF) innovators	136	64.7	48.0	72.8	44.7	89.7	30.5	70.6	45.7	69.1	46.4	47.8	50.1

(continued)

1.4 R&D Outcomes and Inputs

Table 1.7 Determinants of total R&D expenditure

Difference	N	Gross sales in the previous year		Profits in the previous year		R&D expenditure in the previous year		Labor costs of R&D organization(s)		Cumulative costs of individual R&D projects		Annual sales goals for new products as a share of total sales	
		Share (%)	S.E.	Share (%)	S.E.	Share (%)	S.E.	Share (%)	S.E.	Share (%)	S.E.	Share (%)	S.E.
(a)–(b), Small vs. Medium	509	−2.6	4.5	−1.3	4.3	−12.8***	3.5	−6.0	4.3	1.2	4.4	1.2	4.6
(b)–(c), Medium vs. Large	297	−6.7	6.0	−5.4	5.7	−2.9	3.6	−12.7**	5.4	−13.0**	5.8	−2.2	6.1
(a)–(c), Small vs. Large	416	−9.3*	5.6	−6.6	5.3	−15.7***	4.5	−18.6***	5.3	−11.8**	5.4	−1.0	5.7
(d)–(e), Non-innovators vs. Innovators	609	−11.9***	4.0	−11.4***	3.8	−8.6***	3.0	−8.7**	3.8	−5.6	3.9	−5.7	4.1
(e1)–(e2), NTM vs. NTF innovators	193	−10.3	7.7	−7.9	7.2	−7.2	5.2	4.9	7.1	−4.2	7.4	6.6	7.9

Note Figures represent the percentage share of firms that responded with either "fully taken into account" or "to some extent taken into account" when determining total R&D expenditure. ***, **, and * indicate significance at the 1, 5, and 10% levels respectively

firms fully or to some extent take gross sales in the previous year into account, compared to 52.2% of non-innovating firms—a difference of 11.9 percentage points. Similarly, the share of firms that take profits in the previous year into account is 11.4 percentage points higher among innovating firms (72.5%) than non-innovating firms (61.2%). Given that innovating firms are concerned not only about the costs of R&D projects but also their gross sales and profits when deciding their R&D budget, the results suggest that innovating firms are more flexible in adjusting their R&D budget to their performance.

The shares of new-to-market innovators that take either performance-related factors or cost-related factors into account are smaller than those of new-to-firm innovators, except in the case of labor costs and annual sales goals for new products as a share of total sales. However, for all factors, the differences between these two subsamples are not statistically significant.

1.4.3 R&D Inputs: R&D Personnel

Next, we provide an overview of another R&D input: the total number of R&D personnel and their age composition.[14] Table 1.8(a) reports the number of R&D personnel and the ratio to the total number of employees and Table 1.8(b) reports the number of R&D personnel with a doctorate degree and the ratio to the total number of R&D personnel. As in the case when we used the R&D-to-sales ratio in Table 1.5, we use these ratios to adjust for firm size. Table 1.8(a) shows that the mean number of R&D personnel is 74, while the median is 16. The mean of the R&D personnel-to-total-employees ratio is 9.2%, and the median is 5.5%. While we find that the number of R&D employees increases with firm size, no clear pattern in terms of the R&D personnel-to-total-employees ratio can be observed: it is lowest for medium-sized firms (7.7%) and highest for small firms (10.1%).

The mean of the number of R&D personnel is 107 for innovating firms and 35 for non-innovating firms, which means that the total number of R&D employees of innovating firms is 3.1 times larger than that of non-innovating firms. However, the means of the R&D personnel-to-total-employees ratio are approximately nine persons for both subsamples, and the difference between the two is not significant. These results are similar to the patterns observed for R&D expenditure and the R&D expenditure-to-sales ratio in Table 1.5.

The mean of the number of R&D personnel of new-to-market innovators is 3.5 times smaller than that of new-to-firm innovators, while the R&D-to-total-employees ratios are approximately 9% for both subsamples. Interestingly, the latter result is different from that for the R&D expenditure-to-sales ratio in Table 1.5, where we observed that the R&D-to-sales ratio of new-to-market innovators was significantly larger than that of new-to-firm innovators. Taken together, the results in Tables 1.5 and

---

[14] "R&D personnel" in the survey refers to individuals holding at least a bachelor's degree (or having equivalent or greater expertise) and engaged in R&D activities in their area of expertise for more than half of their working hours.

1.4 R&D Outcomes and Inputs

Table 1.8 R&D personnel

(a) R&D personnel

	Number of R&D personnel				Ratio to total employees (%)			
	N	Mean	S.D.	Median	N	Mean	S.D.	Median
Entire sample	611	73.6	262.6	16.0	611	9.2	12.1	5.5
By firm size								
(a) Small	314	11.5	14.4	7.0	314	10.1	13.8	6.0
(b) Medium	195	43.2	66.2	27.0	195	7.7	9.8	4.9
(c) Large	102	322.6	575.3	113.5	102	9.1	9.7	5.4
Non-innovators vs. Innovators								
(d) Non-innovators	278	34.7	81.2	12.0	278	8.7	11.8	5.4
(e) Innovators	331	106.5	345.7	19.0	331	9.3	11.4	5.5
New-to-market vs. New-to-firm innovators								
(e1) New-to-market (NTM) innovators	57	26.9	45.4	11.0	57	8.9	13.8	5.1
(e2) New-to-firm (NTF) innovators	136	94.8	286.8	18.0	136	8.6	10.5	4.7
Difference	N	Mean	S.E.		N	Mean	S.E.	
(a)–(b), Small vs. Medium	509	−31.7***	3.9		509	2.4**	1.1	
(b)–(c), Medium vs. Large	297	−279.4***	41.7		297	−1.4	1.2	
(a)–(c), Small vs. Large	416	−311.1***	32.4		416	0.9	1.5	
(d)–(e), Non-innovators vs. Innovators	609	−71.8***	21.2		609	−0.6	0.9	
(e1)–(e2), NTM vs. NTF innovators	193	−67.9*	38.2		193	0.3	1.8	

(continued)

Table 1.8 R&D personnel

(b) R&D personnel with doctorate degree (Ph.D.)

	N	Number of R&D personnel with Ph.D.			Ratio to total R&D employees (%)			
		Mean	S.D.	Median	N	Mean	S.D.	Median
Entire sample	611	3.9	17.0	0.0	587	5.4	12.5	0.0
By firm size								
(a) Small	314	0.5	1.1	0.0	292	5.8	15.7	0.0
(b) Medium	195	2.7	9.9	0.0	194	4.8	8.6	0.0
(c) Large	102	16.6	36.8	3.0	101	5.5	7.6	2.1
Non-innovators vs. Innovators								
(d) Non-innovators	278	2.9	17.6	0.0	266	5.3	13.5	0.0
(e) Innovators	331	4.7	16.6	0.0	319	5.5	11.7	0.0
New-to-market vs. New-to-firm innovators								
(e1) New-to-market (NTM) innovators	57	1.8	7.2	0.0	52	6.7	18.1	0.0
(e2) New-to-firm (NTF) innovators	136	4.2	13.7	0.0	132	5.5	9.8	0.0
Difference	N	Mean	S.E.		N	Mean	S.E.	
(a)–(b), Small vs. Medium	509	−2.2***	0.6		486	1.0	1.2	
(b)–(c), Medium vs. Large	297	−14.0***	2.8		295	−0.8	1.0	
(a)–(c), Small vs. Large	416	−16.2***	2.1		393	0.2	1.6	
(d)–(e), Non-innovators vs. Innovators	609	−1.8	1.4		585	−0.2	1.0	
(e1)–(e2), NTM vs. NTF innovators	193	−2.4	1.9		184	1.2	2.1	

Note ***, **, and * indicate significance at the 1, 5, and 10% levels respectively

1.4 R&D Outcomes and Inputs

1.8(a) suggest that new-to-market innovators spend more on R&D than new-to-firm innovators, but less of that spending is on R&D personnel.

Table 1.8(b) indicates that the majority of firms in the survey do not employ R&D personnel with doctorate degrees.[15] The mean of the number of Ph.D. researchers is 3.9, while the median is 0, and the mean of the Ph.D. researchers-to-total R&D personnel ratio is 5.4%. Looking at the subsample results, while the average number of Ph.D. researchers is larger for larger firms, the ratio to R&D employees is approximately the same across small, medium, and large firms (5–6%). Similarly, the share of Ph.D. researchers is 5–6% regardless of whether firms are product innovators or not, and whether firms are new-to-market innovators or new-to-firm innovators.

Table 1.9 reports the age composition of R&D personnel. In the sample overall, researchers aged 24–34 years old accounted for 34.9%, those aged 35–44 for 27.2%, and those aged 45 or older for 37.9%. We assume that job roles and titles correspond to researchers' age and refer to R&D personnel aged 24–34 as young researchers, those aged 35–44 as middle or project managers, and those aged 45 or over as chief or division managers. The share of chief or division managers in R&D organizations is highest in small firms (41.4%), while the share of young researchers is lowest in small firms (31.0%).

There is little difference in the age composition of researchers between product innovators or non-innovators: the share of young researchers is around 35% at both product innovators and non-innovators. However, when we compare the share of young researchers between new-to-market innovators and new-to-firm innovators, the share is smaller at the former (29.6%) than the latter (36.9%).

---

[15] The White Paper on Science and Technology 2017 (Ministry of Education, Culture, Sports, Science and Technology) shows that the percentage share of researchers with a Ph.D. in the total R&D personnel in Japanese firms is 4.4% on average, which is lower than the corresponding shares in other OECD countries. For example, the share is 10.1% in U.S firms and 6.7% in Korean firms.

Table 1.9 Age composition of R&D personnel

	N	Young researchers (age: 24–34)		Middle managers (age: 35–44)		Chief managers (age: 45 or over)	
		Mean (Share, %)	S.D.	Mean (Share, %)	S.D.	Mean (Share, %)	S.D.
Entire sample	602	34.9	21.7	27.2	17.6	37.9	23.2
By firm size							
(a) Small	311	31.0	23.4	27.6	21.5	41.4	26.4
(b) Medium	194	40.5	20.3	26.7	13.0	32.8	18.3
(c) Large	97	36.4	15.5	26.8	10.2	36.8	18.3
Non-innovators vs. Innovators							
(d) Non-innovators	275	33.6	22.9	27.4	18.1	39.0	25.0
(e) Innovators	325	36.0	20.7	27.0	17.2	37.0	21.5
New-to-market vs. New-to-firm innovators							
(e1) New-to-market (NTM) innovators	56	29.6	23.2	30.9	26.1	39.5	28.7
(e2) New-to-firm (NTF) innovators	134	36.9	21.5	26.9	16.6	36.1	21.0
Difference	N	Mean (Share, %)	S.E.	Mean (Share, %)	S.E.	Mean (Share, %)	S.E.
(a)–(b), Small vs. Medium	505	−9.5***	2.0	0.9	1.7	8.6***	2.2
(b)–(c), Medium vs. Large	291	4.1*	2.3	−0.1	1.5	−4.0*	2.3
(a)–(c), Small vs. Large	408	−5.4**	2.5	0.8	2.3	4.6	2.9
(d)–(e), Non-innovators vs. Innovators	600	−2.4	1.8	0.4	1.4	2.0	1.9
(e1)–(e2), NTM vs. NTF innovators	190	−7.4**	3.5	4.0	3.2	3.4	3.7

Note ***, **, and * indicate significance at the 1, 5, and 10% levels respectively

1.5 Organizational Structure of R&D Activities

In this section, we discuss the relationship between the organizational design of R&D activities and innovation from the following two perspectives based on our discussion in Sect. 1.2.1. First, we examine whether there is a link between the organizational structure of R&D activities, i.e., whether the R&D structure is centralized or decentralized, and innovation outcomes. In particular, we examine whether there is a link between a centralized R&D structure and explorative (new-to-market) innovation. Second, we examine whether the delegation of authority to R&D organizations promotes innovation.

In our survey, we first asked several questions about the organizational structure of R&D activities, such as the number of R&D organizations within a firm.[16] We then asked whether firms operated a centralized or decentralized R&D structure (Sect. 1.5.1). In cases where firms had a hybrid R&D structure consisting of both centralized and decentralized R&D activities, we also asked about the percentage shares of R&D expenditure and R&D personnel devoted to centralized and decentralized R&D activities (Sect. 1.5.2). Finally, to investigate whether firms delegate authority to R&D organizations, we asked whether it is the R&D organization or the human resources department that takes the initiative in hiring R&D personnel (Sect. 1.5.3).

1.5.1 Centralized/Decentralized R&D Structure

Table 1.10 reports the number of R&D organizations a firm has and whether they are directly controlled by business units or one or more of them are highly independent of business units. The first column indicates that the mean of the number of R&D organizations in the sample overall is 3.3, while the median is 1.0. We find that the number of R&D organizations increases with firm size, and the differences between the different size categories are statistically significant.

The mean of the number of R&D organization is 4.3 for innovating firms and 2.1 for non-innovating firms, which means that the total number of R&D organizations of the former is approximately twice as large as that of the latter. The mean of the number of R&D organizations of new-to-market innovators (2.1) is less than half of that of new-to-firm innovators (5.5), although the difference between the two subsamples is insignificant.

The second to fourth columns of Table 1.10 classify firms in terms of the organizational structure of their R&D activities. Specifically, following Argyres and

---

[16] Using the terminology in Argyres and Silverman (2004; Fig. 2), "R&D organizations" in the survey refers to organizations (such as departments, divisions, or units) in which R&D personnel mainly conduct R&D. For the purpose of the survey, organizations that perform R&D activities are regarded as "R&D organizations" even if their name does not include the words "Research" or "Development."

Table 1.10 R&D organizational structure

	Number of R&D organizations				Organizational structure of R&D activities							
						Highly independent of business units (centralized)		Directly controlled by business units (decentralized)		Both centralized and decentralized R&D entities (hybrid)	
	N	Mean	S.D.	Median	N	Share (%)	S.D.	Share (%)	S.D.	Share (%)	S.D.
Entire sample	609	3.3	11.7	1.0	585	45.3	49.8	41.4	49.3	13.3	34.0
By firm size											
(a) Small	313	1.4	1.1	1.0	298	46.3	49.9	49.0	50.1	4.7	21.2
(b) Medium	195	2.8	2.7	2.0	190	45.3	49.9	41.1	49.3	13.7	34.5
(c) Large	101	9.9	27.5	4.0	97	42.3	49.7	18.6	39.1	39.2	49.1
Non-innovators vs. Innovators											
(d) Non-innovators	278	2.1	2.7	1.0	264	45.8	49.9	45.5	49.9	8.7	28.3
(e) Innovators	329	4.3	15.6	2.0	320	44.7	49.8	38.1	48.6	17.2	37.8
New-to-market vs. New-to-firm innovators											
(e1) New-to-market (NTM) innovators	57	2.1	1.6	1.0	55	49.1	50.5	41.8	49.8	9.1	29.0
(e2) New-to-firm (NTF) innovators	135	5.5	23.5	1.0	131	47.3	50.1	32.1	46.9	20.6	40.6

(continued)

1.5 Organizational Structure of R&D Activities

Table 1.10 R&D organizational structure

Difference	Number of R&D organizations			Organizational structure of R&D activities							
				N	Highly independent of business units (centralized)		Directly controlled by business units (decentralized)		Both centralized and decentralized R&D entities (hybrid)	
	N	Mean	S.E.		Mean	S.E.	Mean	S.E.	Mean	S.E.
(a)–(b), Small vs. Medium	508	−1.4***	0.2	488	1.0	4.6	7.9**	4.6	−9.0***	2.5
(b)–(c), Medium vs. Large	296	−7.1***	2.0	287	3.0	6.2	22.5***	5.8	−25.5***	5.0
(a)–(c), Small vs. Large	414	−8.5***	1.6	395	4.0	5.8	30.4***	5.6	−34.5***	3.6
(d)–(e), Non-innovators vs. Innovators	607	−2.3**	0.9	584	1.1	4.1	7.3*	4.1	−8.5***	2.8
(e1)–(e2), NTM vs. NTF innovators	192	−3.4	3.1	186	1.8	8.1	9.8	7.7	−11.5*	6.0

Note ***, **, and * indicate significance at the 1, 5, and 10% levels respectively

Silverman (2004), we classify firms into the following three categories: firms with a centralized R&D structure, where R&D organizations are highly independent of business units, firms with a decentralized structure, where R&D organizations are directly controlled by business units, and firms with a hybrid structure, i.e., firms that have both a centralized R&D entity (such as a dedicated central R&D facility) and decentralized R&D entities that are embedded in other business units.

The shares of firms in the sample overall that have a centralized, decentralized, or hybrid structure are 45%, 41%, and 13%, respectively. Since the median of the number of R&D organizations in the sample overall is 1.0, this result indicates that the majority of firms in the sample have one R&D organization that is either highly independent of business units or that is directly controlled by a business unit. The percentage share of firms that have a centralized R&D structure is very similar across small, medium, and large firms (42–46%). The share of decentralized structures is highest among small firms (49%), while the share of hybrid structures is highest among large firms (39%).

Innovating firms are more likely to choose a hybrid R&D structure and less likely to choose a decentralized structure. The share of firms that have a decentralized structure is 7 percentage points lower among product innovators (38%) than non-innovators (45%), while the share of firms that have a hybrid structure is 8 percentage points higher among product innovators (17%) than non-innovators (9%). The share of firms that have a centralized R&D structure is about 45% for both subsamples and there is little difference between the two.

We find that most new-to-market innovators do not have a hybrid structure but have either a centralized or decentralized R&D structure. The shares of new-to-market innovators that have a centralized or decentralized R&D structure are 49% and 42%, respectively, while the share of firms that have a hybrid structure is only 9%. This result may reflect the fact that many new-to-market innovators are small firms (Table 1.4), among which the share of firms with a hybrid structure is very small (5%). There is little difference in the share of firms with a centralized R&D structure between new-to-market innovators and new-to-firm innovators. This result is inconsistent with Argyres and Silverman's (2004) finding that firms with a centralized R&D structure were more likely to develop explorative innovations (new-to-market innovations in our case). The difference between our and Argyres and Silverman's (2004) results may be due to differences in the samples used: while 80% of the firms in our sample are small and medium-sized firms, the firms in Argyres and Silverman's (2004) sample were mostly large conglomerate corporations.[17]

Overall, we find that firms that developed product innovations, especially new-to-firm innovations, are more likely to have a hybrid R&D structure. Among firms that made product innovations, we find that most new-to-market innovators have either a

---

[17] Because Argyres and Silverman's (2004) sample consists mostly of large conglomerate corporations, 62.5% of their sample firms have a hybrid R&D structure. Similarly, Argyres et al. (2020) focus on 130 large corporations.

centralized or a decentralized R&D structure. This result is inconsistent with studies (such as Argyres and Silverman 2004) that find that it is firms with a centralized R&D structure that tend to generate radical innovations.

1.5.2 Allocation of R&D Expenditure and R&D Personnel in Firms with a Hybrid R&D Structure

In the case of firms that had a hybrid R&D structure with both centralized and decentralized R&D activities, we additionally asked about the allocation of R&D expenditure and R&D personnel among the two. There are 77 firms that have a hybrid structure in our sample. Because the number of observations is very small, in this subsection we mainly report the summary statistics and do not discuss the statistical significance of differences across different groups.

Table 1.11(a) shows the average number of independent R&D organizations and of dependent R&D organizations that form part of another business unit for the 77 firms that have a hybrid R&D structure. The average number of independent R&D organizations is 2.9, while the median is 1.0. Further, the average number of dependent R&D organizations is 8.7, while the median is 3.0. Thus, the number of dependent R&D organizations is larger than that of independent R&D organizations, presumably because some large firms have many business units. Looking at the median of the sample overall, the typical firm in our sample has four R&D organizations: one independent and three dependent ones.

Large firms have more R&D organizations, and this is reflected primarily in the number of R&D organizations that are part of another business unit. The average number of dependent R&D organizations of large firms (15.3) is 8.5 times larger than that of small firms (1.8), while the average number of independent R&D organizations of large firms (4.4) is 3.6 times larger than that of small firms (1.2).

Turning to innovation, innovating firms have a larger average number of both independent and dependent R&D organizations than non-innovating firms. Looking at the median for the subsample of product innovators, we find that the typical innovating firm has one independent and three or four dependent R&D organizations. Among product innovators, new-to-market innovators have a smaller number of each type of R&D organization than new-to-firm innovators. Looking at the medians, the typical new-to-market innovator has one independent and one dependent R&D organization, while the typical new-to-firm innovator has two independent and four dependent R&D organizations.

Table 1.11(b) reports the percentage shares of R&D expenditure and R&D personnel accounted for by independent R&D organizations at firms with hybrid R&D structures. The mean (median) of the R&D expenditures share of independent R&D organizations is 44.5% (40.0%), while the mean (median) of the R&D personnel share of independent R&D organizations is 40.3% (30.0%). Table 1.11(a)

Table 1.11 R&D activities in firms with a hybrid R&D structure

(a) Number of R&D organizations

	N	Independent organizations			Dependent organizations		
		Mean	S.D.	Median	Mean	S.D.	Median
Entire sample	77	2.9	4.6	1.0	8.7	28.7	3.0
By firm size							
(a) Small	14	1.2	0.8	1.0	1.8	1.2	1.0
(b) Medium	26	1.7	1.3	1.0	3.1	2.8	2.0
(c) Large	37	4.4	6.3	2.0	15.3	40.5	5.0
Non-innovators vs. Innovators							
(d) Non-innovators	23	2.0	2.7	1.0	4.1	5.3	2.0
(e) Innovators	54	3.3	5.3	1.0	10.7	33.9	3.5
New-to-market vs. New-to-firm innovators							
(e1) New-to-market (NTM) innovators	5	1.4	0.5	1.0	1.6	0.9	1.0
(e2) New-to-firm (NTF) innovators	27	3.4	4.0	2.0	16.1	47.4	4.0
Difference	N	Mean	S.E.		Mean	S.E.	
(a)–(b), Small vs. Medium	40	−0.5	0.4		−1.3*	0.8	
(b)–(c), Medium vs. Large	63	−2.7**	1.3		−12.2	8.0	
(a)–(c), Small vs. Large	51	−3.2*	1.7		−13.5	10.9	
(d)–(e), Non-innovators vs. Innovators	77	−1.3	1.2		−6.6	7.1	
(e1)–(e2), NTM vs. NTF innovators	32	−2.0	1.8		−14.5	21.5	

(continued)

1.5 Organizational Structure of R&D Activities

Table 1.11 R&D activities in firms with a hybrid R&D structure

(b) Share of R&D expenditure and R&D personnel of independent R&D organizations

	R&D expenditure				R&D employees			
	N	Mean (Share, %)	S.D.	Median	N	Mean (Share, %)	S.D.	Median
Entire sample	73	44.5	27.6	40.0	76	40.3	26.9	30.0
By firm size								
(a) Small	14	45.8	26.6	45.0	14	41.8	23.1	43.0
(b) Medium	26	48.2	28.5	48.0	26	43.2	26.5	32.0
(c) Large	33	41.0	27.8	33.0	36	37.6	28.9	29.0
Non-innovators vs. Innovators								
(d) Non-innovators	22	38.0	28.3	31.5	23	40.2	28.6	30.0
(e) Innovators	51	47.3	27.1	49.0	53	40.3	26.4	34.0
New-to-market vs. New-to-firm innovators								
(e1) New-to-market (NTM) innovators	5	64.0	18.2	70.0	5	46.2	25.4	50.0
(e2) New-to-firm (NTF) innovators	25	45.9	26.4	49.0	27	37.4	25.1	30.0
Difference	N	Mean (Share, %)	S.E.		N	Mean (Share, %)	S.E.	
(a)–(b), Small vs. Medium	40	−2.4	9.2		40	−1.4	8.4	
(b)–(c), Medium vs. Large	59	7.3	7.4		62	5.6	7.2	
(a)–(c), Small vs. Large	47	4.8	8.8		50	4.2	8.6	
(d)–(e), Non-innovators vs. Innovators	73	−9.2	7.0		76	−0.2	6.8	
(e1)–(e2), NTM vs. NTF innovators	30	18.1	12.4		32	8.8	12.2	

Note ***, **, and * indicate significance at the 1, 5, and 10% levels respectively

showed that the medians of the number of independent and dependent R&D organizations are one and three, respectively so that the percentage share of the number of independent R&D organizations is 25%, which is smaller than the percentage shares of R&D expenditure and R&D personnel. This suggests that, among firms that have a hybrid R&D structure, independent R&D organizations account for more R&D inputs (in terms of expenditure and employees) than dependent R&D organizations.

1.5.3 Initiative in Hiring R&D Personnel

Table 1.12 shows the responses to the question about who takes the initiative in hiring R&D personnel, the R&D organization or the human resources (HR) department.[18] The most frequent answer is both the R&D organization and the HR department (58.1%), followed by the HR department (21.1%), and the R&D organization (15.9%). Thus, in most firms, the R&D organization and the HR department jointly take the initiative in hiring R&D personnel. The pattern is quite similar for small, medium, and large firms. However, one notable finding is that the percentage share of small firms that responded "other" (7.3%) is significantly higher than that of medium-sized and large firms.

The percentage share of firms where both the R&D organization and the HR department take the initiative is significantly higher for innovating firms (62.5%) than for non-innovating firms (52.9%). In contrast, the share of firms where the R&D organization takes the initiative is significantly lower for innovating firms (13.3%) than for non-innovating firms (19.1%). The latter result is inconsistent with studies that found a positive link between the delegation of authority and innovation such as Acemoglu et al. (2007) and Kastl et al. (2013). Among innovating firms, the percentage share of firms where the R&D organization takes the initiative in hiring R&D employees is significantly higher for new-to-market innovators (19.3%) than for new-to-firm innovators (8.8%). This result suggests that there is a positive link between the delegation of authority and explorative innovation and appears consistent with the findings by Acemoglu et al. (2007) and Kastl et al. (2013). Overall, Table 1.12 shows that whether the delegation of authority to R&D organizations is positively associated with innovation depends on the proxy used for innovation, i.e., whether a firm introduced new products in the market, or the type of product innovation (new-to-firm or new-to-market).[19]

---

[18] In Sect. 1.6.1.3 (Table 1.15), we will examine to what extent the authority to manage R&D projects is delegated to R&D organizations.

[19] Although not directly related to the key concern of this monograph—the link between R&D management practices and innovation outcomes—it should be noted that R&D decentralization and the delegation of authority over R&D activities may be closely intertwined, as pointed out in footnote 4 in Sect. 1.2.1. As an aside, we therefore examine whether there is a link between the delegation of authority in hiring R&D personnel to R&D organizations (Table 1.12) and whether firms have a centralized or decentralized R&D structure (Sect. 1.5.1, Table 1.10). We find that the percentage share of firms where the R&D organization takes the initiative in hiring R&D personnel

1.5 Organizational Structure of R&D Activities

Table 1.12 Department that takes the initiative in hiring R&D personnel

	N	R&D organization		HR department		Both R&D and HR		Other	
		Share (%)	S.D.	Share (%)	S.D.	Share (%)	S.D.	Share (%)	S.D.
Entire sample	611	15.9	36.6	21.1	40.8	58.1	49.4	4.9	21.6
By firm size									
(a) Small	314	17.5	38.1	19.8	39.9	55.4	49.8	7.3	26.1
(b) Medium	195	12.3	32.9	25.6	43.8	59.5	49.2	2.6	15.8
(c) Large	102	17.7	38.3	16.7	37.5	63.7	48.3	2.0	13.9
Non-innovators vs. Innovators									
(d) Non-innovators	278	19.1	39.4	21.6	41.2	52.9	50.0	6.5	24.7
(e) Innovators	331	13.3	34.0	20.9	40.7	62.5	48.5	3.3	18.0
New-to-market vs. New-to-firm innovators									
(e1) New-to-market (NTM) innovators	57	19.3	39.8	17.5	38.4	57.9	49.8	5.3	22.5
(e2) New-to-firm (NTF) innovators	136	8.8	28.5	22.1	41.6	64.7	48.0	4.4	20.6
Difference	N	Share (%)	S.E.	Share (%)	S.E.	Share (%)	S.E.	Share (%)	S.E.
(a)–(b), Small vs. Medium	509	5.2	3.3	−5.9	3.8	−4.1	4.5	4.8**	2.1
(b)–(c), Medium vs. Large	297	−5.3	4.3	9.0*	5.1	−4.2	6.0	0.6	1.9
(a)–(c), Small vs. Large	416	−0.1	4.3	3.1	4.5	−8.3	5.6	5.4**	2.7
(d)–(e), Non-innovators vs. Innovators	609	5.8*	3.0	0.7	3.3	−9.7**	4.0	3.2*	1.7
(e1)–(e2), NTM vs. NTF innovators	193	10.5**	5.1	−4.5	6.4	−6.8	7.7	0.9	3.3

Note ***, **, and * indicate significance at the 1, 5, and 10% levels respectively

1.6 R&D Project Management

This section investigates how R&D projects are managed. Specifically, we examine whether and how staged project management, in which the project proceeds in consecutive multiple stages, is implemented. Based on the discussion and literature review (e.g., Manso 2011) in Sect. 1.2.2, we focus on the threat of termination and feedback in staged project management.

We first provide an overview of the ongoing R&D projects of firms in the sample, including the number of projects and their track record, i.e., whether they were suspended, terminated, or continued (Sect. 1.6.1). We then examine whether and how firms implement staged project management (Sect. 1.6.2). In particular, for firms that implement staged project management, we examine whether firms set milestones in assessing whether an R&D project should be continued and, if they do, how important these milestones are in assessing whether the R&D project is continued (Sect. 1.6.2.1). We also examine whether firms provide feedback to R&D personnel in charge of the project, and if so, whose opinions are incorporated in the feedback (Sect. 1.6.2.2).

1.6.1 Overview on R&D Projects

1.6.1.1 Number of R&D Projects

Table 1.13 reports the approximate number of R&D projects in progress. The mean of the number of ongoing projects for the whole sample is 23.9, while the median is 6.0. Because it is likely that the number of R&D projects is positively correlated with firm size, we also calculate the ratio of the number of ongoing projects to 100 employees (which we refer to as the project-to-employee ratio). The mean of the project-to-employee ratio is 6.9 and the median is 2.3.

Table 1.13 shows that while the number of ongoing projects increases with firm size as expected, the project-to-employee ratio does not and is lowest for medium-sized firms (2.9) and highest for small firms (10.5). These patterns are similar to

---

is 20.0% for firms with a centralized R&D structure while it is 14.1% for firms with a decentralized R&D structure. Further, the difference between the subsamples is weakly significant, indicating that in firms with a centralized R&D structure R&D organizations have greater authority in hiring employees. While this result suggests that R&D decentralization and delegation of authority to R&D organizations capture the same aspect of the organization of R&D activities, our analyses also showed that the empirical link between the organizational structure of R&D activities and innovation outcomes presented in Sect. 1.5.1 is different from the empirical link between the delegation of authority over R&D activities and innovation outcomes presented in this subsection (Sect. 1.5.3). We therefore think that it is safe to assume that the delegation of authority in hiring R&D personnel to R&D organizations and whether R&D activities are centralized or decentralized captures different aspects of the organization of R&D activities.

1.6 R&D Project Management

Table 1.13 Number of R&D projects in progress

	N	Number of ongoing R&D projects			Project-to-employee ratio		
		Mean	S.D.	Median	Mean	S.D.	Median
Entire sample	600	23.9	66.8	6.0	6.9	26.8	2.3
By firm size							
(a) Small	311	9.6	20.2	4.0	10.5	36.6	3.9
(b) Medium	193	15.2	19.8	10.0	2.9	4.0	1.6
(c) Large	96	87.6	145.3	32.5	3.4	5.7	1.4
Non-innovators vs. Innovators							
(d) Non-innovators	275	15.8	57.4	4.0	6.5	27.3	1.9
(e) Innovators	324	30.8	73.3	10.0	7.3	26.4	2.7
New-to-market vs. New-to-firm innovators							
(e1) New-to-market (NTM) innovators	57	11.6	15.5	6.0	7.1	11.4	3.1
(e2) New-to-firm (NTF) innovators	133	26.7	73.0	8.0	4.4	5.5	2.3
Difference	N	Mean	S.E.		Mean	S.E.	
(a)–(b), Small vs. Medium	504	−5.7***	1.8		7.6***	2.6	
(b)–(c), Medium vs. Large	289	−72.4***	10.6		−0.5	0.6	
(a)–(c), Small vs. Large	407	−78.0***	8.5		7.1*	3.8	
(d)–(e), Non-innovators vs. Innovators	599	−14.9***	5.5		−0.9	2.2	
(e1)–(e2), NTM vs. NTF innovators	190	−15.1	9.8		2.8**	1.2	

Notes The project-to-employee ratio represents the number of ongoing projects per 100 employees. ***, **, and * indicate significance at the 1, 5, and 10% levels respectively

those in Table 1.5 for the R&D expenditure-to-sales ratio and Table 1.8 for the R&D personnel-to-total-employees ratio.

The mean of the number of projects in progress is 30.8 for product innovators and 15.8 for non-innovators. However, the mean of the project-to-employee ratio is 7.3 for the former and 6.5 for the latter, and there is no significant difference between the two subsamples. Among product innovators, the mean of the number of ongoing R&D projects for new-to-market innovators (11.6) is less than half of that for new-to-firm innovators (26.7), but the difference is statistically insignificant. By contrast, the mean of the project-to-employee ratio for new-to-market innovators (7.1) is 1.6 times higher for new-to-firm innovators (4.4), and the difference between the subsamples is statistically significant. This result indicates that, once we adjust for firm size, new-to-market innovators undertake a larger number of R&D projects than new-to-firm innovators, presumably because new-to-market innovations require more experimentation.

1.6.1.2 Duration of R&D Projects

Next, we turn to the duration of R&D projects, about which the survey asked two questions. First, it asked about the average number of years from the commencement of a project to the achievement of final results. And second, it asked about the approximate share of current R&D projects that have continuously been ongoing for more than three years. Table 1.14 presents the results.

The mean of the average duration of R&D projects of firms in the entire sample is 3.5 years. Meanwhile, the mean of the percentage share of current R&D projects that had been in progress for more than three years is 38.7%, which is in line with the finding that the average duration is 3.5 years.

Looking at various subsamples, the means of the average duration of R&D projects are quite similar for small and medium firms, product innovators and non-innovators, and new-to-market innovators and new-to-firm innovators. The one subsample whose mean, at 3.9 years, is slightly larger than that of other firms is large firms, which compares to 3.4 years for small and medium-sized firms. Similar patterns are observed when looking at the percentage share of R&D projects that had been ongoing for more than three years: we find no significant differences among the various subsamples.

1.6.1.3 Termination or Suspension of R&D Projects

Table 1.15 reports whether a firm has any R&D projects that had been terminated or suspended within the past three years (first column) and the approximate share of projects where R&D organizations have the authority to decide whether to terminate, suspend, or continue the project (right column). The table shows that 59.5% of firms

1.6 R&D Project Management

Table 1.14 Duration of R&D projects

	Average number of year from the commencement of an R&D project to the achievement of final results				Share of R&D projects that have continuously been on going for more than 3 years			
	N	Mean	S.D.	Median	N	Mean (Share, %)	S.D.	Median
Entire sample	597	3.5	2.5	3.0	565	38.7	31.9	33.0
By firm size								
(a) Small	309	3.4	2.5	3.0	290	36.6	32.5	30.0
(b) Medium	191	3.4	2.1	3.0	182	40.3	31.6	33.0
(c) Large	97	3.9	2.8	3.0	93	42.2	30.4	40.0
Non-innovators vs. Innovators								
(d) Non-innovators	271	3.5	2.6	3.0	249	39.1	32.9	33.0
(e) Innovators	326	3.4	2.3	3.0	315	38.6	31.1	33.0
New-to-market vs. New-to-firm innovators								
(e1) New-to-market (NTM) innovators	57	3.6	2.3	3.0	56	36.1	30.3	33.0
(e2) New-to-firm (NTF) innovators	133	3.5	2.0	3.0	127	41.1	31.5	37.0
Difference	N	Mean	S.E.		N	Mean (Share, %)	S.E.	
(a)–(b), Small vs. Medium	500	0.0	0.2		472	−3.7	3.0	
(b)–(c), Medium vs. Large	288	−0.5*	0.3		275	−1.9	4.0	
(a)–(c), Small vs. Large	406	−0.6*	0.3		383	−5.6	3.8	
(d)–(e), Non-innovators vs. Innovators	597	0.1	0.2		564	0.5	2.7	
(e1)–(e2), NTM vs. NTF innovators	190	0.1	0.3		183	−5.0	5.0	

Note ***, **, and * indicate significance at the 1, 5, and 10% levels respectively

Table 1.15 Termination or suspension of R&D projects

	Firms with projects that were terminated/suspended within the past 3 years				Share of projects where R&D organizations have the authority to decide whether to terminate, suspend, or continue the project			
	N	Share (%)	S.D.		N	Mean (Share, %)	S.D.	Median
Entire sample	603	59.5	49.1		564	40.8	40.9	30.0
By firm size								
(a) Small	312	51.9	50.0		288	39.3	41.5	25.0
(b) Medium	193	61.7	48.7		182	43.1	41.3	30.0
(c) Large	98	79.6	40.5		94	40.8	38.4	30.0
Non-innovators vs. Innovators								
(d) Non-innovators	277	50.9	50.1		248	39.6	41.2	25.0
(e) Innovators	325	67.1	47.1		316	41.7	40.8	30.0
New-to-market vs. New-to-firm innovators								
(e1) New-to-market (NTM) innovators	57	59.7	49.5		56	45.2	43.8	50.0
(e2) New-to-firm (NTF) innovators	134	64.2	48.1		128	40.6	41.1	29.0
Difference	N	Mean	S.E.		N	Mean (Share, %)	S.E.	
(a)–(b), Small vs. Medium	410	−9.7**	4.5		470	−3.8	3.9	
(b)–(c), Medium vs. Large	291	−17.9***	5.7		276	2.3	5.1	
(a)–(c), Small vs. Large	410	−27.7***	5.6		382	−1.5	4.8	
(d)–(e), Non-innovators vs. Innovators	602	−16.2***	4.0		564	−2.1	3.5	
(e1)–(e2), NTM vs. NTF innovators	191	−4.5	7.7		184	4.6	6.7	

Note ***, **, and * indicate significance at the 1, 5, and 10% levels respectively

1.6 R&D Project Management

in the whole sample had terminated and/or suspended at least one of their R&D projects within past three years. We find that the share of firms that had terminated or suspended an R&D project clearly increases with firm size, presumably because larger firms have a larger number of ongoing R&D projects (Table 1.13).

The share of firms that had terminated and/or suspended projects is significant higher for innovating firms (67.1%) than non-innovating firms (50.9%). This suggests that innovating firms face challenges during the product development process more frequently than non-innovating firms, resulting in a higher likelihood of termination/suspension. However, when we look at the shares for new-to-market innovators (59.7%) and new-to-firm innovators (64.2%), we find that it is slightly lower for new-to-market innovators. Because new-to-market innovators are more likely to face challenges than new-to-firm innovators, this finding is inconsistent with our interpretation above that innovating firms are more likely to terminate or suspend projects because they face challenges more frequently. We infer that innovating firms are more likely to terminate/suspend projects because both the share of innovating firms (Table 1.3) and the share of firms that had terminated or suspended an R&D project (Table 1.15) increases with firm size. This inference is consistent with the observation that the share of new-to-market innovators is highest among small firms, whereas the share of new-to-firm innovators is smallest among small firms (Table 1.4).

In Sect. 1.5.3, we examined to what extent R&D organizations have the authority to hire R&D employees (Table 1.12). In Table 1.15, we examine the delegation of authority to R&D organizations from a different angle. Specifically, we examine the share of projects in a firm where the R&D organization has the authority to decide whether to terminate/suspend or continue the project. We find that the mean of this share is 40.8% (median: 30.0%). Looking at the different subsamples, the shares are approximately 40% for small, medium, and large firms, and for product innovators and non-innovators. Among innovators, the share is slightly higher for new-to-market innovators (45.2%) than for new-to-firm innovators (40.6%), but the difference between the two is insignificant. In contrast to Table 1.12, where we observed that the percentage share of firms whose R&D organizations had the initiative to hire R&D personnel is higher for new-to-market innovators than for new-to-firm innovators, there is no difference between the two in terms of R&D organizations' authority to decide on the continuation of projects.

1.6.2 Staged Project Management

In the survey, we define staged project management as "a method of R&D project management in which the project proceeds in consecutive multiple stages (phases)."[20] Table 1.16(a) shows the percentage shares of firms that implement staged project management for R&D projects. Moreover, firms that employed staged project management were asked to provide more details, including the average number of stages, whether they set intermediate goals (milestones) for the interim evaluation of projects, and whether they provide feedback on the interim evaluation results to R&D personnel in charge of the project. The results for these additional questions are shown in Table 1.16(b).

The percentage share of firms that employ staged project management is 51.3% (313 firms). We find that the likelihood of employing staged project management is higher for larger firms. The share of innovating firms that employed staged project management (64.7%) is higher than that of non-innovating firms (35.6%), suggesting that there is a positive link between staging and making product innovation. Among innovating firms, the share is 59.6% for new-to-market innovators and 57.4% for new-to-firm innovators. The difference between the two subsamples is small and insignificant.

Turning to the average number of stages in Table 1.16(b), we find that the mean of the average number of stages for the whole sample is 4.6. It is slightly larger for large firms (5.2) than for small firms (4.1). The differences between product innovators and non-innovators and between new-to-market product innovators and new-to-firm product innovators are small and insignificant.

Next, we look at the shares of firms that set milestones for interim evaluation and that provide feedback on the evaluation results to R&D personnel. Among firms that employ staged project management, 78.6% set milestones for interim evaluation, and 85.3% provide feedback on the interim evaluation results to R&D personnel. Large firms are more likely to set milestones: the share of large firms that set milestones (93.3%) is significantly higher than those of medium (79.3%) and small firms (69.7%). However, we find that the provision of feedback does not increase with firm size.

The share of firms that set milestones is significantly higher among product innovators (81.3%) than non-innovators (72.7%). In addition, the share of firms that provide feedback is also significantly higher among product innovators (88.8%) than non-innovators (77.6%). Among product innovators, the share that set milestones is similar for new-to-market (79.4%) and new-to-firm innovators (78.2%). The share of firms that provide feedback is slightly higher for new-to-market innovators (88.2%) than new-to-firm innovators (82.1%), but the difference between the subsamples is insignificant.

---

[20] Specifically, in the glossary of terms sent to respondents (see the Appendix), we defined staged project management as follows:

> "Staged project management" refers to the management of R&D projects in consecutive stages, such as "ideation and concept development," "preliminary assessment of commercialization," "development," "testing and validation," and "production and marketing." Staged project management also entails a phase-based interim evaluation that affects the decision about whether the project is continued, suspended, or abandoned, as well as a revision of the schedule.

1.6 R&D Project Management

Table 1.16 Staged project management

(a) Share of firms that implement staged project management

	Staged project management		
	N	Share (%)	S.D.
Entire sample	610	51.3	50.0
By firm size			
(a) Small	314	42.0	49.4
(b) Medium	194	54.6	49.9
(c) Large	102	73.5	44.3
Non-innovators vs. Innovators			
(d) Non-innovators	278	35.6	48.0
(e) Innovators	331	64.7	47.9
New-to-market vs. New-to-firm innovators			
(e1) New-to-market (NTM) innovators	57	59.6	49.5
(e2) New-to-firm (NTF) innovators	136	57.4	49.6
Difference	N	Mean	S.E.
(a)–(b), Small vs. Medium	508	−12.6***	4.5
(b)–(c), Medium vs. Large	296	−18.9***	5.9
(a)–(c), Small vs. Large	416	−31.5***	5.5
(d)–(e), Non-innovators vs. Innovators	609	−29.0***	3.9
(e1)–(e2), NTM vs. NTF innovators	193	2.3	7.8

(continued)

Table 1.16 Staged project management

(b) Number of stages, milestones, and feedback

	Number of stages				Intermediate goals for the interim evaluation of projects (milestones)			Feedback on the interim evaluation results		
	N	Mean	S.D.	Median	N	Share (%)	S.D.	N	Share (%)	S.D.
Entire sample	305	4.6	4.2	4	313	78.6	41.1	312	85.3	35.5
By firm size										
(a) Small	130	4.1	2.3	4	132	69.7	46.1	131	86.3	34.6
(b) Medium	105	4.7	4.2	4	106	79.3	40.7	106	82.1	38.5
(c) Large	70	5.2	6.4	4	75	93.3	25.1	75	88.0	32.7
Non-innovators vs. Innovators										
(d) Non-innovators	97	4.3	4.4	3	99	72.7	44.8	98	77.6	41.9
(e) Innovators	208	4.7	4.1	4	214	81.3	39.1	214	88.8	31.6
New-to-market vs. New-to-firm innovators										
(e1) New-to-market (NTM) innovators	34	5.1	4.5	5	34	79.4	41.0	34	88.2	32.7
(e2) New-to-firm (NTF) innovators	76	4.6	4.5	4	78	78.2	41.6	78	82.1	38.6
Difference	N	Mean	S.E.		N	Mean	S.E.	N	Mean	S.E.
(a)–(b), Small vs. Medium	235	−0.5	0.4		238	−9.5*	5.7	237	4.2	4.8
(b)–(c), Medium vs. Large	175	−0.5	0.8		181	−14.1***	5.3	181	−5.9	5.5
(a)–(c), Small vs. Large	200	−1.1*	0.6		207	−23.6***	5.8	206	−1.7	4.9
(d)–(e), Non-innovators vs. Innovators	305	−0.4	0.5		313	−8.6*	5.0	312	−11.2***	4.3
(e1)–(e2), NTM vs. NTF innovators	110	0.5	0.9		112	1.2	8.5	112	6.2	7.6

Note The sample consists of firms that implement staged project management. ***, **, and * indicate significance at the 1, 5, and 10% levels respectively

1.6 R&D Project Management

To sum up, we find that firms that succeed in making product innovations are more likely to manage R&D projects in stages, set milestone for interim evaluation, and provide feedback on a project's interim evaluation results to researchers. These results are consistent with the literature highlighting the positive effects of staging in R&D projects (Cooper 1988, 2017) and VC investments (Sahlman 1990; Gompers 1995; Kaplan and Strömberg 2003). We do not find any differences between new-to-market innovators and new-to-firm innovators. In particular, we do not find evidence suggesting that staging deters firms from engaging in explorative R&D projects. In the following subsections, we examine the role of milestones and feedback in more detail.

1.6.2.1 Milestones

As noted, firms that employ staged project management were asked a number of further questions. In addition to whether they set milestones (Table 1.16), we also asked how important these milestones were for successfully completing a project. Specifically, we divided project management stages into "initial stages" (e.g., idea/basic research) and "late stages" (e.g., preparation for launching new goods/services) and asked to what extent firms took into account whether milestones were achieved when assessing whether to terminate/suspend or continue the R&D project.

Table 1.17 reports the results for the importance of milestones, with panel (a) showing those for initial stages and panel (b) those for late stages. In the initial stages, 28.0% of firms "fully" take into account whether milestones were achieved in deciding whether to terminate/suspend or continue an R&D project. In contrast, in late stages, 63.0% of firms fully take milestones into account. These results indicate that the achievement of milestones is more important in late stages than in initial stages. In addition, if we assume that firms that "fully" take the achievement of milestones into account for initial stages are firms that employ "the threat of termination" (Manso 2011) as a way to manage their R&D projects, our result suggests that 28.0% of Japanese firms use such threat of termination. Another notable feature in Table 1.17 is that the share of firms that answered "not very much" or "not at all" to the question of whether they take milestones into account is 10.9% (8.9 + 2.0) for the initial stages. This suggests that about 10% of firms in our sample have "tolerance for early failure" (Manso 2011). For comparison, the corresponding share for later stages 2.4% (2.0 + 0.4).

Next, using firms that "fully" take milestones into account and firms that take milestones "not very much" or "not at all" into account, we examine whether and how "the threat of termination" and "tolerance for early failure" is linked to innovation outcomes. The shares of firms in which R&D projects face the threat of termination (i.e., milestones are "fully taken into account" in the initial stages) and the shares of firms that have a tolerance for early failure (the sum of firms saying milestones are "not very much taken into account" or "not taken into account at all" in the initial

Table 1.17 Importance of milestones

(a) Initial stages

	N	Fully taken into account		To some extent taken into account		Not very much taken into account		Not taken into account at all	
		Share (%)	S.D.	Share (%)	S.D.	Share (%)	S.D.	Share (%)	S.D.
Entire sample	246	28.0	45.0	61.0	48.9	8.9	28.6	2.0	14.1
By firm size									
(a) Small	92	26.1	44.2	65.2	47.9	7.6	26.7	1.1	10.4
(b) Medium	84	25.0	43.6	64.3	48.2	8.3	27.8	2.4	15.3
(c) Large	70	34.3	47.8	51.4	50.3	11.4	32.0	2.9	16.8
Non-innovators vs. Innovators									
(d) Non-innovators	72	22.2	41.9	68.1	47.0	8.3	27.8	1.4	11.8
(e) Innovators	174	30.5	46.2	58.1	49.5	9.2	29.0	2.3	15.0
New-to-market vs. New-to-firm innovators									
(e1) New-to-market (NTM) innovators	27	22.2	42.4	59.3	50.1	14.8	36.2	3.7	19.2
(e2) New-to-firm (NTF) innovators	61	26.2	44.4	62.3	48.9	9.8	30.0	1.6	12.8
Difference	N	Share (%)	S.E.	Share (%)	S.E.	Share (%)	S.E.	Share (%)	S.E.
(a)–(b), Small vs. Medium	176	1.1	6.6	0.9	7.2	−0.7	4.1	−1.3	2.0
(b)–(c), Medium vs. Large	154	−9.3	7.4	12.9	8.0	−3.1	4.8	−0.5	2.6
(a)–(c), Small vs. Large	162	−8.2	7.3	13.8*	7.8	−3.8	4.6	−1.8	2.1
(d)–(e), Non-innovators vs. Innovators	246	−8.2	6.3	10.0	6.8	−0.9	4.0	−0.9	2.0
(e1)–(e2), NTM vs. NTF innovators	88	−4.0	10.1	−3.0	11.4	5.0	7.4	2.1	3.5

(continued)

1.6 R&D Project Management

Table 1.17 Importance of milestones

(b) Late stages

	N	Fully taken into account		To some extent taken into account		Not very much taken into account		Not taken into account at all	
		Share (%)	S.D.	Share (%)	S.D.	Share (%)	S.D.	Share (%)	S.D.
Entire sample	246	63.0	48.4	34.6	47.7	2.0	14.1	0.4	6.4
By firm size									
(a) Small	92	59.8	49.3	35.9	48.2	4.3	20.5	0.0	0.0
(b) Medium	84	60.7	49.1	39.3	49.1	0.0	0.0	0.0	0.0
(c) Large	70	70.0	46.2	27.1	44.8	1.4	12.0	1.4	12.0
Non-innovators vs. Innovators									
(d) Non-innovators	72	56.9	49.9	38.9	49.1	4.2	20.1	0.0	0
(e) Innovators	174	65.5	47.7	32.8	47.1	1.1	10.7	0.6	7.6
New-to-market vs. New-to-firm innovators									
(e1) New-to-market (NTM) innovators	27	63.0	49.2	33.3	48.0	3.7	19.2	0.0	0.0
(e2) New-to-firm (NTF) innovators	61	60.7	49.3	39.3	49.3	0.0	0.0	0.0	0.0
Difference	N	Share (%)	S.E.	Share (%)	S.E.	Share (%)	S.E.	Share (%)	S.E.
(a)–(b), Small vs. Medium	176	−0.9	7.4	−3.4	7.3	4.3*	2.2	0.0	0.0
(b)–(c), Medium vs. Large	154	−9.3	7.7	12.1	7.6	−1.4	1.3	−1.4	1.3
(a)–(c), Small vs. Large	162	−10.2	7.6	8.7	7.4	2.9	2.8	−1.4	1.2
(d)–(e), Non-innovators vs. Innovators	246	−8.6	6.8	6.1	6.7	3.0	2.0	−0.6	0.9
(e1)–(e2), NTM vs. NTF innovators	88	2.3	11.4	−6.0	11.3	3.7	2.4	0.0	0.0

Note Figures represent the share of firms that ticked a particular answer in response to the following question: "To what extent do you take into account whether intermediate goals (milestones) were achieved when assessing whether to terminate/suspend or continue the R&D project?" ***, **, and * indicate significance at the 1, 5, and 10% levels respectively

stages) are similar among small, medium, and large firms; between product innovators and non-innovators; and between new-to-market and new-to-firm innovators. For example, the share of firms that fully take milestones into account in the initial stages is 22.2% for new-to-market innovators, while it is 26.2% for new-to-firm innovators. This seems consistent with Manso's (2011) argument that the threat of termination promotes exploitation, but the difference between the two subsamples is insignificant. Similarly, the share of firms that take milestone not very much or not at all into account in the initial stages is 18.5% (14.8 + 3.7) for new-to-market innovators, while it is 11.4% (9.8 + 1.6) for new-to-firm innovators. Again, this seems consistent with Manso's (2011) argument that tolerance for early failure promotes exploration, but the difference between the two is insignificant. Overall, we do not find evidence that the threat of termination and/or tolerance for early failure affects the likelihood of engaging in explorative (new-to-market) innovation. Our results are consistent with Manso's (2011) theoretical prediction that whether the threat of termination is beneficial or detrimental to exploration is ambiguous but inconsistent with empirical findings by Ederer and Manso (2013) and Mao et al. (2014), who find that the threat of termination is detrimental to exploration.

Finally, it should be noted that to what extent a firm considers the achievement of milestones in deciding whether to continue an R&D project may be associated not only with the extent to which firms employ the threat of termination in their project management and with their tendency to tolerate early failure, but may also be linked to other factors. For example, a firm that engages in a joint research project with other firms (external partners) may put greater emphasis on the achievement of milestones to comply with contracts governing such joint research. Other factors such as receiving funds from VC investors, who usually invest in stages and set milestones for their investment, may also be positively associated with the extent to which the achievement of milestones is taken into account. Therefore, to examine whether and how the threat of termination and tolerance for early failure are associated with innovation outcomes requires proper statistical analysis, which we leave for future studies.

1.6.2.2 Feedback

Further, as mentioned, in the case of firms that employ staged project management, we also asked about feedback to researchers. Table 1.18 reports the results for the question about whose opinions are incorporated when providing feedback on the interim evaluation results to R&D employees. In the survey questionnaire, we provided three possible, not mutually exclusive options: "Opinions from other research teams within R&D organizations," "opinions from non-R&D organizations (business units and head office) within the company," and "opinions (including informal ones) from external experts outside the company." We again divided project management stages into initial and late stages and asked respondents in which stages these opinions were incorporated. A firm may, for example, incorporate opinions from other research teams within R&D organizations for both the initial and late stages (multiple answers

1.6 R&D Project Management

Table 1.18 Feedback on interim evaluation results: Opinions that are incorporated

(a) Opinions from other research teams in the same or other R&D organizations

	N	Incorporated in initial stages			Incorporated in late stages			Not incorporated		
		Share (%)	S.D.		Share (%)	S.D.		Share (%)	S.D.	
Entire sample	266	70.7	45.6		55.3	49.8		24.4	43.1	
By firm size										
(a) Small	113	70.8	45.7		55.8	49.9		25.7	43.9	
(b) Medium	87	73.6	44.4		59.8	49.3		20.7	40.7	
(c) Large	66	66.7	47.5		48.5	50.4		27.3	44.9	
Non-innovators vs. Innovators										
(d) Non-innovators	76	72.4	45.0		57.9	49.7		22.4	41.9	
(e) Innovators	190	70.0	45.9		54.2	50.0		25.3	43.6	
New-to-market vs. New-to-firm innovators										
(e1) New-to-market (NTM) innovators	30	66.7	47.9		46.7	50.7		30.0	46.6	
(e2) New-to-firm (NTF) innovators	64	67.2	47.3		50.0	50.4		29.7	46.0	
Difference	N	Share (%)	S.E.		Share (%)	S.E.		Share (%)	S.E.	
(a)–(b), Small vs. Medium	200	−2.8	6.4		−4.0	7.1		5.0	6.1	
(b)–(c), Medium vs. Large	153	6.9	7.5		11.3	8.1		−6.6	6.9	
(a)–(c), Small vs. Large	179	4.1	7.2		7.3	7.8		−1.6	6.9	
(d)–(e), Non-innovators vs. Innovators	266	2.4	6.2		3.7	6.8		−2.9	5.9	
(e1)–(e2), NTM vs. NTF innovators	94	−0.5	10.5		−3.3	11.2		0.3	10.2	

(continued)

Table 1.18 Feedback on interim evaluation results: Opinions that are incorporated

(b) Opinions from non-R&D organizations (business units and head office) within the company

	N	Incorporated in initial stages		Incorporated in late stages		Not incorporated	
		Share (%)	S.D.	Share (%)	S.D.	Share (%)	S.D.
Entire sample	266	70.7	45.6	83.8	36.9	5.3	22.4
By firm size							
(a) Small	113	73.5	44.4	84.1	36.8	2.7	16.1
(b) Medium	87	74.7	43.7	81.6	39.0	5.8	23.4
(c) Large	66	60.6	49.2	86.4	34.6	9.1	29.0
Non-innovators vs. Innovators							
(d) Non-innovators	76	61.8	48.9	88.2	32.5	2.6	16.1
(e) Innovators	190	74.2	43.9	82.1	38.4	6.3	24.4
New-to-market vs. New-to-firm innovators							
(e1) New-to-market (NTM) innovators	30	83.3	37.9	83.3	37.9	6.7	25.4
(e2) New-to-firm (NTF) innovators	64	71.9	45.3	84.4	36.6	4.7	21.3
Difference	N	Share (%)	S.E.	Share (%)	S.E.	Share (%)	S.E.
(a)–(b), Small vs. Medium	200	−1.3	6.3	2.5	5.4	−3.1	2.8
(b)–(c), Medium vs. Large	153	14.1*	7.5	−4.8	6.1	−3.3	4.2
(a)–(c), Small vs. Large	179	12.8*	7.2	−2.3	5.6	−6.4*	3.4
(d)–(e), Non-innovators vs. Innovators	266	−12.4**	6.2	6.1	5.0	−3.7	3.0
(e1)–(e2), NTM vs. NTF innovators	94	11.5	9.5	−1.0	8.2	2.0	5.0

(continued)

1.6 R&D Project Management

Table 1.18 Feedback on interim evaluation results: Opinions that are incorporated

(c) Opinions (including informal ones) from external experts outside the company

	N	Incorporated in initial stages		Incorporated in late stages		Not incorporated	
		Share (%)	S.D.	Share (%)	S.D.	Share (%)	S.D.
Entire sample	266	30.0	45.9	24.7	43.2	62.4	48.5
By firm size							
(a) Small	113	31.8	46.8	26.4	44.3	60.0	49.2
(b) Medium	87	26.4	44.4	24.1	43.0	65.5	47.8
(c) Large	66	31.8	46.9	22.7	42.2	62.1	48.9
Non-innovators vs. Innovators							
(d) Non-innovators	76	29.3	45.8	25.3	43.8	62.7	48.7
(e) Innovators	190	30.3	46.1	24.5	43.1	62.2	48.6
New-to-market vs. New-to-firm innovators							
(e1) New-to-market (NTM) innovators	30	36.7	49.0	46.7	50.7	46.7	50.7
(e2) New-to-firm (NTF) innovators	64	26.6	44.5	23.4	42.7	67.2	47.3
Difference	N	Share (%)	S.E.	Share (%)	S.E.	Share (%)	S.E.
(a)–(b), Small vs. Medium	200	5.4	6.6	2.2	6.3	−5.5	7.0
(b)–(c), Medium vs. Large	153	−5.4	7.4	1.4	7.0	3.4	7.9
(a)–(c), Small vs. Large	179	0.0	7.3	3.6	6.8	−2.1	7.6
(d)–(e), Non-innovators vs. Innovators	266	−1.0	6.3	0.9	5.9	0.4	6.6
(e1)–(e2), NTM vs. NTF innovators	94	10.1	10.2	23.2**	10.0	−20.5*	10.7

Note ***, **, and * indicate significance at the 1, 5, and 10% levels respectively

allowed). If a firm did not incorporate specific opinions in any of the stages, we asked firms to answer with "not incorporated."

Table 1.18 reports the results. The most frequent answer regarding whose opinions are incorporated is non-R&D organizations within the company (Table 1.18(b), initial stage: 70.7%, late stage: 83.8%), followed by other research teams within R&D organizations (Table 1.18(a), initial: 70.7%, late: 55.3%), and external experts outside the company (Table 1.18(c), initial: 30.0%, late: 24.7%). We find that the share of firms that incorporate opinions from external experts is the smallest among the three options, and 62.4% of firms in the sample do not incorporate opinions from external experts outside the company at all. Comparing the stage when opinions are incorporated into feedback, we find that opinions from other teams within R&D organizations and those from non-R&D organizations are equally incorporated in the initial stages, whereas opinions from the latter are more likely to be incorporated in the late stages. These results suggest that firms' main concern is the technological feasibility of product ideas when a project is launched, and as the project progresses, concern gradually shifts to commercialization of the invention and product marketing.

Looking at the subsample results in Table 1.18(b), the share of firms that incorporate opinions from non-R&D organizations in the initial stages is smallest among large firms (60.6%). In addition, the share of firms that do not incorporate opinions from non-R&D organizations is highest among large firms (9.1%). These results suggest that large firms tend to not incorporate opinions from non-R&D organizations, presumably because they have a vertically segmented organizational structure. Next, comparing product innovators and non-innovators, the share of firms that incorporate opinions from non-R&D organizations in the initial stages is significantly higher among innovating firms (74.2%) than among non-innovating firms (61.8%). This suggests that opinions from non-R&D organizations are important for making product innovations.

Looking at the subsample results in Table 1.18(c), we find that the share of firms that incorporate opinions from external experts is higher among new-to-market innovators (initial: 36.7%, late: 46.7%) than new-to-firm innovators (initial: 26.6%, late: 23.4%). In addition, the share of firms that do not incorporate opinions from external experts is significantly higher among new-to-firm innovators (67.2%) than new-to-market innovators (46.7%). These results are consistent with Manso's (2011) theoretical prediction that timely feedback on interim performance promotes explorative innovation and Azoulay et al.'s (2011) finding that detailed and high-quality feedback from experts leads researchers to produce higher-impact scientific articles.

While we found a positive link between seeking feedback from external experts and new-to-market innovation, we note that there may be other factors that affect from whom a firm seeks feedback. For instance, firms that obtain funding from VC investors are more likely to have feedback from external experts, because VC investors usually provide "value-added services" such as strategic and operational guidance (Gompers et al. 2020). Another example is small firms, which make up a sizable share of new-to-market innovators (Table 1.4) and may seek advice from outside experts to compensate for a lack of experts within the firm.

1.7 Evaluation of R&D Personnel

This section, based on our discussion in Sect. 1.2.3, examines how firms design compensation contracts and incentive schemes to increase their R&D personnel's motivation for innovation.

We begin with an overview of salary schemes employed for R&D personnel (Sect. 1.7.1). We then look more deeply into compensation contracts and incentive schemes for R&D personnel. First, we examine to what extent Japanese firms use performance-based evaluations (Sect. 1.7.2). Specifically, in Sect. 1.7.2.1, we focus on the relative weights assigned to ability and performance in the evaluation of a young R&D employee.[21] In addition, in Sect. 1.7.2.2, we consider the criteria firms use for the evaluation of R&D personnel. We use firms' responses to examine whether there is a negative association between performance-based evaluation and the likelihood of innovation (as suggested, e.g., by Holmström and Milgrom 1991) or a positive association (as suggested by Prendergast 2002 and Foss and Laursen 2005). Second, we look at what kinds of pecuniary and non-pecuniary incentives firms offer to R&D personnel and examine whether there is a link between these incentives and innovation (Sect. 1.7.3). Third, we examine long-term incentives for R&D employees from two different perspectives (Sect. 1.7.4). Specifically, in Sect. 1.7.4.1, we revisit some of the questions used in Sects. 1.7.2.2 and 1.7.3. and regard the following two items as incentives for long-term success: whether a firm employs the amount of sales generated by new products as an evaluation criterion for the long-term success of R&D personnel (see Table 1.21 in Sect. 1.7.2.2), and whether a firm employs invention reward schemes as incentives for long-term success (see Table 1.22 in Sect. 1.7.3). In Sect. 1.7.4.2, we focus on another potential long-term incentive for innovation: the possibility of promotion of R&D personnel to top management levels. Specifically, we ask firms whether a person that belonged to an R&D organization in the past became a director on the board of the firm.

1.7.1 Salary Schemes for R&D Personnel

We conducted pre-interviews with several Japanese firms that actively engaged in R&D activities and found that the majority of Japanese firms employ the same salary schemes for their R&D personnel as for other employees. Based on this finding, we asked firms what kind of salary scheme they employed for R&D personnel and whether it was different from the salary schemes for other employees (multiple choices allowed).

Table 1.19 reports the results for this question. We find that the most frequent

---

[21] In the survey, we define "ability" as a person's potential ability to perform their duties (e.g., willingness and attitude, cognitive ability, and interpersonal skills). We define "performance" as a person's results achieved in performing their duties. The results evaluated include, for example, patent applications, prototype products, and commercialization.

Table 1.19 Salary schemes for R&D personnel

	N	A specific salary scheme for R&D personnel		Starting salary varies depending on the educational background		Salary scheme based on performance-based pay		R&D personnel can choose from among various schemes		None of the schemes listed are employed	
		Share (%)	S.D.	Share (%)	S.D.	Share (%)	S.D.	Share (%)	S.D.	Share (%)	S.D.
Entire sample	608	8.1	27.2	72.5	44.7	14.6	35.4	2.1	14.5	18.1	38.5
By firm size											
(a) Small	313	10.2	30.3	66.5	47.3	14.1	34.8	1.6	12.6	21.7	41.3
(b) Medium	194	7.7	26.8	77.3	42.0	17.5	38.1	2.1	14.2	13.9	34.7
(c) Large	101	2.0	14.0	82.2	38.5	10.9	31.3	4.0	19.6	14.9	35.7
Non-innovators vs. Innovators											
(d) Non-innovators	278	8.6	28.1	70.1	45.8	11.5	32.0	1.4	11.9	19.8	39.9
(e) Innovators	329	7.6	26.5	74.5	43.7	17.3	37.9	2.7	16.3	16.7	37.4
New-to-market vs. New-to-firm innovators											
(e1) New-to-market (NTM) innovators	57	8.8	28.5	63.2	48.7	14.0	35.0	1.8	13.2	22.8	42.3
(e2) New-to-firm (NTF) innovators	135	4.4	20.7	77.8	41.7	15.6	36.4	0.7	8.6	14.8	35.7

(continued)

1.7 Evaluation of R&D Personnel

Table 1.19 Salary schemes for R&D personnel

Difference	N	A specific salary scheme for R&D personnel		Starting salary varies depending on the educational background		Salary scheme based on performance-based pay		R&D personnel can choose from among various schemes		None of the schemes listed are employed	
		Share (%)	S.E.	Share (%)	S.E.	Share (%)	S.E.	Share (%)	S.E.	Share (%)	S.E.
(a)–(b), Small vs. Medium	507	2.5	2.7	−10.9***	4.1	−3.5	3.3	−0.5	1.2	7.8**	3.6
(b)–(c), Medium vs. Large	295	5.8**	2.8	−4.9	5.0	6.6	4.4	−1.9	2.0	−0.9	4.3
(a)–(c), Small vs. Large	414	8.2***	3.1	−15.7***	5.2	3.2	3.9	−2.4	1.7	6.9	4.6
(d)–(e), Non-innovators vs. Innovators	607	1.0	2.2	−4.3	3.6	−5.8**	2.9	−1.3	1.2	3.1	3.1
(e1)–(e2), NTM vs. NTF innovators	192	4.3	3.7	−14.6**	6.9	−1.5	5.7	1.0	1.6	8.0	6.0

Note Respondents were asked to choose all that apply. ***, **, and * indicate significance at the 1, 5, and 10% levels respectively

answer is that the "starting salary varies depending on the educational background" (72.5%). Because such education-based salary schemes are widely used among firms in Japan not only for R&D personnel but also for other employees, the result is consistent with the finding in our pre-interviews. The second most frequent answer is that the firm uses a "salary system based on performance-based pay" (14.6%), followed by "a specific salary scheme for R&D personnel that differs from that for other employees" (8.1%) and "R&D personnel can choose from among various salary schemes" (2.1%). Meanwhile, 18.1% of firms in the sample answered that "none of the salary schemes listed above are employed." Because the percentage shares of firms that use a performance-based salary scheme and a specific salary scheme for R&D personnel are relatively low, we infer that the majority of Japanese firms do not provide pay-for-performance compensation schemes for R&D employees.

Looking at the subsample results, we find that larger firms are more likely to employ education-based salary schemes. The share is highest for large firms (82.2%) and lowest for small firms (66.5%). In contrast, the share of firms that provide a specific salary scheme for R&D personnel is lowest for large firms (2.0%) and highest for small firms (10.2%).

The share of firms that employ a performance-based salary system is significantly higher for product innovators (17.3%) than for non-innovators (11.5%). Although the share of firms that employ a performance-based salary scheme is less than 20% even among product innovators, this finding suggests that there is a positive association between performance-based pay and product innovations. Meanwhile, there is little difference between product innovators and non-innovators in terms of the other salary schemes that we listed.

Among product innovators, the share of firms that employ an education-based salary scheme is significantly lower for new-to-market innovators (63.2%) than for new-to-firm innovators (77.8%). Because education-based salary schemes are widely used among Japanese firms, the lower ratio for new-to-market innovators may suggest that they are more likely to employ other salary schemes including performance-based compensation schemes. However, the results in Table 1.19 do not bear this out: the differences between new-to-market and new-to-firm innovators with regard to the use of performance-based pay or R&D personnel-specific schemes are small and insignificant.

Finally, the share of firms that answered "none of the schemes above are employed" is higher among new-to-market innovators (22.8%) than for new-to-firm innovators (14.8%), which suggests that new-to-market innovators are more likely to employ salary schemes not listed in our survey, but the difference between the two is again insignificant. Overall, while we find that new-to-market innovators are less likely to employ education-based salary schemes, we cannot pin down which salary schemes they are more likely to employ for R&D personnel.

1.7.2 Performance- and Ability-Based Evaluation

1.7.2.1 Weights on Performance and Ability in Evaluation

In this subsection, we focus on the results for the question about the weight firms put on "ability" and "performance" when evaluating R&D personnel in their early 30s. Table 1.20 shows the results for the weight put on performance (the results for ability are omitted to save space since the two weights add up to 100%). The mean of the approximate weight firms put on performance is 46.4%, while the mean of the weight on ability is 53.6%.

Looking at subsamples, we observe several differences across firm groups in terms of the weight they put on performance. First, while the means of the weight on performance are quite similar across small, medium, and large firms, large firms put a somewhat higher weight on performance (49.3%) than small firms (44.8%) and this difference is significant. Second, product innovators put a significantly higher weight on performance than non-innovators: the mean of the weight is 47.9% for product innovators and 44.6% for non-innovators. This suggests that there is a positive link

Table 1.20 Weight put on performance in employee evaluation

	N	Mean (%)	S.D.	Median
Entire sample	599	46.4	18.1	50.0
By firm size				
(a) Small	308	44.8	18.5	50.0
(b) Medium	192	47.4	16.9	50.0
(c) Large	99	49.3	18.6	50.0
Non-innovators vs. Innovators				
(d) Non-innovators	274	44.6	18.1	50.0
(e) Innovators	325	47.9	17.9	50.0
New-to-market vs. New-to-firm innovators				
(e1) New-to-market (NTM) innovators	57	46.0	18.8	50.0
(e2) New-to-firm (NTF) innovators	133	47.6	18.7	50.0
Difference	N	Mean (%)	S.E.	
(a)–(b), Small vs. Medium	500	−2.6	1.6	
(b)–(c), Medium vs. Large	291	−2.0	2.2	
(a)–(c), Small vs. Large	407	−4.5**	2.1	
(d)–(e), Non-innovators vs. Innovators	599	−3.3**	1.5	
(e1)–(e2), NTM vs. NTF innovators	190	−1.6	3.0	

Note Figures represent the weight that respondent firms put on performance as opposed to ability in the evaluation of an R&D employee in their early 30s. "Performance" refers to the level of achievement met in performing the job, while "ability" refers to the abilities demonstrated in performing the job. ***, **, and * indicate significance at the 1, 5, and 10% levels respectively

between product innovation and performance-based evaluation.[22] Together with the positive link between product innovation and performance-based salary schemes in Table 1.19, these results are consistent with Foss and Laursen's (2005) finding of a positive link between innovation and the use of performance pay.[23] Finally, among product innovators, we do not find a significant difference between new-to-market and new-to-firm innovators.

1.7.2.2 Criteria for the Evaluation of R&D Personnel

Table 1.21 presents results regarding the criteria that firms employ for the evaluation of R&D personnel (multiple choices allowed). The survey provided seven criteria as possible choices. Two of the criteria are related to the ability of R&D personnel, namely, "research papers and conference presentations" and "acquisition of qualifications/degree." The other four criteria are related to their performance, namely, "patent applications/registrations," "commercialization (launch) of new products," "amount of sales generated by new products to which the R&D employee contributed," and "R&D progress, including compliance with a schedule."

We find that the most widely used criterion is "R&D progress" (71.5%). The shares of firms using the other criteria are relatively similar. In descending order, they are "acquisition of qualifications/degrees" (18.6%), "amount of sales generated by new products" (14.7%), "commercialization of new products" (14.7%), "patent applications/registrations" (9.6%), and "research papers and presentations" (4.4%). The share of firms answering that "none of the criteria listed above are employed" is 8.1%. These figures indicate that the share of the most frequently cited performance-related criterion (R&D progress) is about four times as large as the share of the most frequently cited ability-related criterion (acquisition of qualification/degree). This suggests that most firms in the sample are likely to employ performance- rather than ability-related criteria for the evaluation of R&D employees. That said, it should

---

[22] We note that such a positive link between product innovation and performance-based evaluation could be due to the positive link between product innovation and firm size on the one hand and the positive link between the weight put on performance and firm size on the other hand.

[23] Note that while we find evidence of a positive link between product innovation and the use of performance pay, in this monograph we do not examine the reasons for such a link. A possible explanation is provided by Prendergast (2002), who argues that there may be a positive link between the use of pay-for-performance and uncertainty (i.e., innovation, in our case) since in uncertain environments, a principal (manager) delegates responsibility to agents (employees) and uses performance-based pay to compensate for agents' unobservable effort (see Sect. 1.2.3). To check whether the positive link between the weight firms put on performance in their evaluation of employees and product innovation we find in Table 1.20 is consistent with Prendergast's (2002) argument, we examine the link between the delegation of authority in hiring R&D personnel to R&D organizations (Table 1.12) and the weight put on performance (Table 1.20). However, we find that the mean of the weight on performance is almost identical between firms that delegate the initiative in hiring R&D personnel to R&D organizations and firms that do not. Similarly, we do not find a positive link between delegation and the likelihood of employing a performance-based salary scheme in Table 1.19. Investigating the mechanism through which product innovation is positively linked to performance is an issue we leave for future research.

1.7 Evaluation of R&D Personnel

Table 1.21 Criteria for the evaluation of R&D personnel

	N	Ability-related criteria				Performance-related criteria								None of the criteria listed are employed	
		Research papers and conference presentations		Acquisition of qualifications / degrees		Patent applications / registrations		Commercialization (Launch) of new products		Amount of sales generated by new products to which the R&D employee contributed		R&D progress, including compliance with schedule			
		Share (%)	S.D.	Share (%)	S.D.	Share (%)	S.D.	Share (%)	S.D.	Share (%)	S.D.	Share (%)	S.D.	Share (%)	S.D.
Entire sample	607	4.4	20.6	18.6	39.0	9.6	29.4	14.7	35.4	14.7	35.4	71.5	45.2	8.1	27.3
By firm size															
(a) Small	313	3.5	18.4	17.9	38.4	8.9	28.6	17.9	38.4	15.3	36.1	67.1	47.1	10.2	30.3
(b) Medium	193	4.1	20.0	14.0	34.8	9.8	29.9	10.9	31.2	14.5	35.3	76.7	42.4	5.7	23.2
(c) Large	101	7.9	27.1	29.7	45.9	10.9	31.3	11.9	32.5	12.9	33.7	75.2	43.4	5.9	23.8
Non-innovators vs. Innovators															
(d) Non-innovators	278	4.3	20.4	15.8	36.6	9.0	28.7	15.8	36.6	15.1	35.9	66.9	47.1	11.2	31.5
(e) Innovators	328	4.6	20.9	20.7	40.6	10.1	30.1	13.7	34.5	14.3	35.1	75.3	43.2	5.5	22.8
New-to-market vs. New-to-firm innovators															
(e1) New-to-market (NTM) innovators	57	7.0	25.8	12.3	33.1	15.8	36.8	17.5	38.4	17.5	38.4	68.4	46.9	7.0	25.8
(e2) New-to-firm (NTF) innovators	134	3.7	19.0	20.1	40.3	6.7	25.1	11.2	31.6	14.2	35.0	75.4	43.2	7.5	26.4

(continued)

Table 1.21 Criteria for the evaluation of R&D personnel

Difference	N	Ability-related criteria				Performance-related criteria								None of the criteria listed are employed	
		Research papers and conference presentations		Acquisition of qualifications / degrees		Patent applications / registrations		Commercialization (Launch) of new products		Amount of sales generated by new products to which the R&D employee contributed		R&D progress, including compliance with schedule			
		Share (%)	S.E.	Share (%)	S.E.	Share (%)	S.E.	Share (%)	S.E.	Share (%)	S.E.	Share (%)	S.E.	Share (%)	S.E.
(a)–(b), Small vs. Medium	506	−0.6	1.7	3.9	3.4	−0.9	2.7	7.0**	3.3	0.8	3.3	−9.6	4.1	4.5*	2.5
(b)–(c), Medium vs. Large	294	−3.8	2.8	−15.7***	4.8	−1.0	3.7	−1.0	3.9	1.6	4.3	1.4	5.2	−0.2	2.9
(a)–(c), Small vs. Large	414	−4.4*	2.4	−11.8**	4.6	−1.9	3.3	6.0	4.2	2.5	4.1	−8.2	5.3	4.3	3.3
(d)–(e), Non-innovators vs. Innovators	606	−0.3	1.7	−4.9	3.2	−1.1	2.4	2.1	2.9	0.8	2.9	−8.4**	3.7	5.7**	2.2
(e1)–(e2), NTM vs. NTF innovators	191	3.3	3.4	−7.9	6.1	9.1**	4.6	6.3	5.3	3.4	5.7	−7.0	7.0	−0.4	4.1

Note Respondents were asked to choose all that apply. ***, **, and * indicate significance at the 1, 5, and 10% levels respectively

be noted that R&D progress, including whether an R&D employee complies with a schedule, may not be a clear-cut criterion of employees' performance since it does not reflect the outcome of their R&D activities.

Large firms tend to utilize a variety of performance- and ability-related criteria for evaluation. Specifically, the shares of large firms using ability-related criteria are significantly higher than those of small firms: the percentage share of firms using "research papers/presentations" is 7.9% for large firms and 3.5% for small firms, while the percentage share of firms using "acquisition of qualifications/degrees" is 29.7% for large firms and 17.9% for small firms.

Similarly, product innovators are more likely to employ both ability- and performance-related criteria, as the share of firms that replied "none of the - criteria listed are employed" is significantly smaller among product innovators (5.5%) than non-innovators (11.2%). Specifically, the share of firms using "R&D progress" is significantly higher among product innovators (75.3%) than non-innovators (66.9%). Among product innovators, the share of firms using "patent applications/registrations" is significantly higher among new-to-market innovators (15.8%) than new-to-firm innovators (6.7%). Again, this result is consistent with the positive link between the use of performance pay and innovation found by Foss and Laursen (2005). A larger share of new-to-market innovators use "commercialization of new products" and "research papers/presentations" as criteria, although the differences between new-to-firm innovators with regard to these criteria are statistically insignificant.

1.7.3 Incentive Schemes for R&D Personnel

Next, we turn to incentive schemes for R&D personnel. The survey provided a list of six different types of incentives—three pecuniary and three non-pecuniary incentives—and asked respondents to tick those that the firm employed (multiple choices allowed). The non-pecuniary incentives were "in-house research presentations," "dispatch to university and/or support for studying abroad," and "open recruitment for R&D projects," while the pecuniary incentives were "awards for outstanding R&D results," "rewards based on the number of patent applications" (referred to as "patent-based rewards" hereinafter), and "rewards based on the amount of profits from inventions and patents (invention reward schemes)."

Table 1.22 shows that the two most widely used incentives are "patent-based rewards" (49.6%) and "invention reward schemes" (44.8%). In descending order, the percentage shares of the other incentives are "awards for outstanding R&D results" (16.4%), "in-house research presentations" (10.5%), "dispatch to university/abroad" (4.8%), and "open recruitment for R&D projects" (1.6%). Meanwhile, 21.7% of sample firms responded that "none of the schemes above are employed." These results indicate that among firms that employ at least one of the listed incentive schemes, pecuniary incentive schemes such as patent-based rewards and invention reward schemes are more likely to be employed than non-pecuniary incentive schemes.

Table 1.22 Incentive schemes for R&D personnel

	N	Non-pecuniary (intrinsic) incentives								Pecuniary (extrinsic) incentives							None of the schemes listed are employed	
		In-house research presentations		Dispatch to university and/or support for studying abroad		Open recruitment for R&D projects		Awards for outstanding R&D results		Rewards based on the number of patent applications		Rewards based on the amount of profits from inventions and patents (invention reward system)					
		Share (%)	S.D.	Share (%)	S.D.	Share (%)	S.D.	Share (%)	S.D.	Share (%)	S.D.	Share (%)	S.D.	Share (%)	S.D.		
Entire sample	609	10.5	30.7	4.8	21.3	1.6	12.7	16.4	37.1	49.6	50.0	44.8	49.8	21.7	41.2		
By firm size																	
(a) Small	313	9.3	29.0	3.5	18.4	2.2	14.8	16.9	37.6	37.4	48.5	31.3	46.4	33.9	47.4		
(b) Medium	194	14.4	35.2	4.6	21.1	1.0	10.1	17.5	38.1	58.8	49.4	54.6	49.9	8.8	28.3		
(c) Large	102	6.9	25.4	8.8	28.5	1.0	9.9	12.7	33.5	69.6	46.2	67.6	47.0	8.8	28.5		
Non-innovators vs. Innovators																	
(d) Non-innovators	278	10.8	31.1	4.3	20.4	1.4	11.9	15.1	35.9	41.7	49.4	37.4	48.5	28.8	45.4		
(e) Innovators	329	10.3	30.5	5.2	22.2	1.8	13.4	17.6	38.2	56.2	49.7	50.8	50.1	15.8	36.5		
New-to-market vs. New-to-firm innovators																	
(e1) New-to-market (NTM) innovators	57	1.8	13.2	0.0	0.0	3.5	18.6	21.1	41.1	47.4	50.4	45.6	50.3	22.8	42.3		
(e2) New-to-firm (NTF) innovators	134	10.4	30.7	6.7	25.1	1.5	12.2	17.2	37.8	55.2	49.9	50.7	50.2	20.1	40.3		

(continued)

1.7 Evaluation of R&D Personnel

Table 1.22 Incentive schemes for R&D personnel

Difference	N	Non-pecuniary (intrinsic) incentives						Pecuniary (extrinsic) incentives						None of the schemes listed are employed	
		In-house research presentations		Dispatch to university and/or support for studying abroad		Open recruitment for R&D projects		Awards for outstanding R&D results		Rewards based on the number of patent applications		Rewards based on the amount of profits from inventions and patents (invention reward system)			
		Share (%)	S.E.	Share (%)	S.E.	Share (%)	S.E.	Share (%)	S.E.	Share (%)	S.E.	Share (%)	S.E.	Share (%)	S.E.
(a)–(b), Small vs. Medium	507	−5.2*	2.9	−1.1	1.8	1.2	1.2	−0.6	3.5	−21.4***	4.5	−23.3***	4.4	25.1***	3.8
(b)–(c), Medium vs. Large	296	7.6*	3.9	−4.2	2.9	0.1	1.2	4.8	4.5	−10.8*	5.9	−13.0**	6.0	−0.1	3.5
(a)–(c), Small vs. Large	415	2.4	3.2	−5.3**	2.4	1.3	1.6	4.2	4.2	−32.2***	5.5	−36.3***	5.3	25.0***	5.0
(d)–(e), Non-innovators vs. Innovators	607	0.5	2.5	−0.9	1.7	−0.4	1.0	−2.5	3.0	−14.5***	4.0	−13.3***	4.0	13.0***	3.3
(e1)–(e2), NTM vs. NTF innovators	191	−8.7***	4.2	−6.7**	3.3	2.0	2.3	3.9	6.1	−7.9	7.9	−5.1	7.9	2.7	6.5

Note Respondents were asked to choose all that apply. ***, **, and * indicate significance at the 1, 5, and 10% levels respectively

Looking at subsamples, larger firms are more likely to employ patent-based rewards and invention reward schemes. For example, the share of large firms that employ patent-based rewards (69.6%) is significantly higher than those of small and medium firms (37.4% and 58.8%, respectively). Among non-pecuniary incentives, the share of firms that use "in-house research presentations" is significantly higher for medium-sized firms (14.4%) than for small firms (9.3%) and large firms (6.9%). Meanwhile, 33.9% of small firms used "none of the incentive schemes listed above," suggesting that small firms employ other incentives not listed in the questionnaire or did not provide any incentives at all.

We find that product innovators are more likely to employ at least one of the incentive schemes listed in the questionnaire: the share of product innovators that replied "none of the schemes above are employed" is 15.8%, while that of non-innovators is 28.8%. Consistent with this finding, the share of firms using a particular incentive scheme is larger for product innovators than innovators for all schemes except in-house research presentations. In particular, the share of product innovators that employ patent-based rewards (56.2%) is significantly higher than that of non-innovators (41.7%). Similarly, the share of product innovators that employ invention reward schemes (50.8%) is significantly higher than that of non-innovators (37.4%).

Among product innovators, we find that new-to-market innovators are less likely to employ non-pecuniary incentive schemes than new-to-firm innovators. The shares of new-to-market innovators that use "in-house research presentations" (1.8%) and "dispatch to university/studying abroad" (0.0%) are significantly lower than those of new-to-firm innovators (10.4% and 6.7%, respectively). Turning to pecuniary incentives, the shares of new-to-market innovators that use patent-based rewards (47.4%) and invention reward schemes (45.6%) are also lower than those of new-to-firm innovators (55.2% and 50.7%, respectively), but the differences between new-to-market and new-to-firm innovators are insignificant.

To sum up, we found that product innovators are more likely to employ pecuniary incentives than non-innovators. This result is consistent with studies such as Onishi (2013) and Sauermann and Cohen (2010) but inconsistent with studies that found a negative link between pecuniary incentives and innovation (e.g., Onishi et al. 2021). Regarding non-pecuniary incentives, we do not find any associations between non-pecuniary incentive schemes and product innovation. This finding is inconsistent with Sauermann and Cohen (2010), who find a positive link between non-pecuniary motives (i.e., preference for intellectual challenge and independence) and innovation (i.e., the number of patent applications). However, among product innovators, we find that new-to-firm innovators are more likely to employ non-pecuniary incentives than new-to-market innovators. This finding indicates that the link between non-pecuniary incentive schemes and innovation outcomes depends on how innovation is measured.

1.7.4 Incentives for Long-Term Success

1.7.4.1 Rewards for Long-Term Success

To examine the role of incentives for long-term success, we focus on the following two items already discussed in Sects. 1.7.2.2 and 1.7.3: the "amount of sales generated by new products to which the R&D employee contributed," which was one of the options in the question on criteria used for the evaluation of R&D personnel (Table 1.21), and "rewards based on the amount of profits from inventions and patents (invention reward schemes)," which was one of the options in the question on incentive schemes for R&D personnel (Table 1.22). In the sections above, we used these items to examine whether a firm focused more on ability or performance in the evaluation of R&D personnel (Sect. 1.7.2.2) and whether a firm used pecuniary or non-pecuniary incentives (Sect. 1.7.3). In this subsection, we revisit these two items to examine whether firms employ rewards for long-term success since it takes time for product innovations to result in sales or profits.

Table 1.23 shows that 14.7% of sample firms employ "the sales amount generated by new products" for the evaluation of R&D personnel. As discussed with regard to Table 1.21, the share of firms using this criterion is not notably higher than the share of other criteria, presumably because it is difficult to measure a single person's contribution to the introduction of a new product. In terms of the share of firms using this criterion, there are no significant differences among small, medium, and large firms, between product innovators and non-innovators, and between new-to-market and new-to-firm innovators.

Next, turning to invention reward schemes, Table 1.23 shows that 44.8% of sample firms employ such schemes as part of their incentive for R&D personnel. Larger firms are more likely to employ invention reward schemes: the share is 67.6% for large firms, 54.6% for medium firms, and 31.3% for small firms. Similarly, product innovators (50.8%) are more likely to employ invention reward schemes than non-innovators (37.4%). Among product innovators, the share of firms that employ invention reward schemes is slightly lower for new-to-market innovators (45.6%) than for new-to-firm innovators (50.7%), but the difference between the two is insignificant.

To summarize, we find that product innovators are more likely to employ invention reward schemes than non-innovators, but we do not find a positive link between the "amount of sales generated by new products to which the R&D employee contributed" and product innovation. This suggests that whether rewards for long-term success contribute to making product innovation depends on the specific tool that a firm employs. We do not find evidence that new-to-market innovators are more likely to use rewards for long-term success than new-to-firm innovators.

Table 1.23 Rewards for long-term success

	Amount of sales generated by new products			Rewards based on the amount of profits from inventions and patents (invention reward system)		
	N	Share (%)	S.D.	N	Share (%)	S.D.
Entire sample	607	14.7	35.4	609	44.8	49.8
By firm size						
(a) Small	313	15.3	36.1	313	31.3	46.4
(b) Medium	193	14.5	35.3	194	54.6	49.9
(c) Large	101	12.9	33.7	102	67.6	47.0
Non-innovators vs. Innovators						
(d) Non-innovators	278	15.1	35.9	278	37.4	48.5
(e) Innovators	328	14.3	35.1	329	50.8	50.1
New-to-market vs. New-to-firm innovators						
(e1) New-to-market (NTM) innovators	57	17.5	38.4	57	45.6	50.3
(e2) New-to-firm (NTF) innovators	134	14.2	35.0	134	50.7	50.2
Difference	N	Share (%)	S.E.	N	Share (%)	S.E.
(a)–(b), Small vs. Medium	506	0.8	3.3	507	−23.3***	4.4
(b)–(c), Medium vs. Large	294	1.6	4.3	296	−13.0**	6.0
(a)–(c), Small vs. Large	414	2.5	4.1	415	−36.3***	5.3
(d)–(e), Non-innovators vs. Innovators	606	0.8	2.9	607	−13.3***	4.0
(e1)–(e2), NTM vs. NTF innovators	191	3.4	5.7	191	−5.1	7.9

Note The results for "Amount of sales generated by new products" are reproduced from Table 1.21, while the results for "Rewards based on the amount of profits from inventions and patents (invention reward system)" are reproduced from Table 1.22. ***, **, and * indicate significance at the 1, 5, and 10% levels respectively

1.7 Evaluation of R&D Personnel

1.7.4.2 Possibility of Promotion

The survey examines another potential incentive for R&D personnel for long-term success: the possibility of promotion. As discussed in Sect. 1.7.3, promotion is a typical reward for long-term success. In the survey, we asked whether any of the directors on the board (e.g., chairperson, president, vice president) belonged to an R&D organization in the past. For the majority of Japanese firms, some board members are internally promoted from among employees who have worked at the firm for a long time. Given this, the possibility that an R&D employee could potentially be nominated as a director on the board may work as a long-term incentive for rank-and-file R&D personnel.

Table 1.24 shows that 38.3% of survey firms have at least one director on the board who belonged to an R&D organization in the past. Looking at subsamples, there are no significant differences among small (37.6%), medium (37.9%), and large (41.2%) firms. Meanwhile, product innovators are more likely to have directors on the board who belonged to an R&D organization than non-innovators. The share of firms that have a board member from an R&D organization is 42.6% among product innovators, while it is 33.1% among non-innovators, and the difference between the

Table 1.24 Directors on the board from R&D organizations

	N	Share (%)	S.D.
Entire sample	611	38.3	48.7
By firm size			
(a) Small	314	37.6	48.5
(b) Medium	195	37.9	48.7
(c) Large	102	41.2	49.5
Non-innovators vs. Innovators			
(d) Non-innovators	278	33.1	47.1
(e) Innovators	331	42.6	49.5
New-to-market vs. New-to-firm innovators			
(e1) New-to-market (NTM) innovators	57	40.4	49.5
(e2) New-to-firm (NTF) innovators	136	41.9	49.5
Difference	N	Share (%)	S.E.
(a)–(b), Small vs. Medium	509	−0.4	4.4
(b)–(c), Medium vs. Large	297	−3.2	6.0
(a)–(c), Small vs. Large	416	−3.6	5.6
(d)–(e), Non-innovators vs. Innovators	609	−9.5**	3.9
(e1)–(e2), NTM vs. NTF innovators	193	−1.6	7.8

Note The table shows the share of firms that have a director on the board that belonged to an R&D organization in the past. ***, **, and * indicate significance at the 1, 5, and 10% levels respectively

two subsamples is significant. Among product innovators, we find no differences between the share for new-to-market innovators (40.4%) and new-to-firm innovators (41.9%).

To summarize, the results in this subsection and Sect. 1.7.4.1 indicate that product innovators are more likely to employ invention reward schemes and have a director on the board who belonged to an R&D organization than non-innovators. This suggests that long-term incentives may be effective in promoting product innovations. However, we do not find evidence that new-to-market innovators are more likely to employ incentive schemes for long-term success than new-to-market innovators. This result does not support Manso's (2011) argument that reward for long-term success is essential for motivating exploration.

1.8 Risk Preferences and Corporate Culture

Recent studies show that firms' risk preferences and corporate culture are important determinants of their risk-taking, including investment in R&D, as discussed in Sect. 1.2.4. In this section, we examine how firms' risk preferences and corporate culture are linked with innovation outcomes.

In Sect. 1.8.1, we provide an overview of the results for three questions that try to capture firms' risk preferences. First, the survey directly asked whether respondents felt that their firm is taking appropriate risk in R&D projects. Second, it set a hypothetical question about an R&D project and asked about the maximum amount that a firm would invest in this project to indirectly infer firms' risk preferences. Third, it asked respondent firms to choose between two otherwise identical projects: one that has a greater NPV but negative cash flow for the first few years and another that has a smaller NPV but positive cash flow throughout its duration. In Sect. 1.8.2, we measure firms' corporate culture by employing the CVF (Cameron et al. 2014) introduced in Sect. 1.2.4, which categorizes corporate culture into the following quadrants: *Collaborate*, *Control*, *Compete*, and *Create*.

1.8.1 Risk Preferences

Table 1.25 shows the results for the following question: "Do you think your R&D organization is taking appropriate risks in R&D projects to achieve its goals?" This question tries to capture firms' subjective risk preferences based on respondents' own judgement. Among the 606 firms that responded to this question, 60 firms (13.2%) chose "Do not know." We exclude these firms, resulting in 526 observations used for Table 1.25.

We find that 68.4% of respondents in the sample believe that their firm takes an appropriate level of risk, 23.4% believe that their firm does not take much risk, and 8.2% believe that their firm takes too much risk. These results are similar to those

1.8 Risk Preferences and Corporate Culture

Table 1.25 Risk preferences: Respondents' assessment of their firm's taking of risk

	N	Does not take much risk		Takes appropriate level of risk		Takes too much risk	
		Share (%)	S.D.	Share (%)	S.D.	Share (%)	S.D.
Entire sample	526	23.4	42.4	68.4	46.5	8.2	27.4
By firm size							
(a) Small	259	20.8	40.7	73.7	44.1	5.4	22.7
(b) Medium	176	27.8	44.9	61.9	48.7	10.2	30.4
(c) Large	91	22.0	41.6	65.9	47.7	12.1	32.8
Non-innovators vs. Innovators							
(d) Non-innovators	233	27.0	44.5	63.9	48.1	9.0	28.7
(e) Innovators	293	20.5	40.4	72.0	45.0	7.5	26.4
New-to-market vs. New-to-firm innovators							
(e1) New-to-market (NTM) innovators	51	13.7	34.8	82.4	38.5	3.9	19.6
(e2) New-to-firm (NTF) innovators	115	27.0	44.6	65.2	47.8	7.8	27.0
Difference	N	Share (%)	S.E.	Share (%)	S.E.	Share (%)	S.E.
(a)–(b), Small vs. Medium	267	−7.0*	4.1	11.8***	4.5	−4.8*	2.5
(b)–(c), Medium vs. Large	267	5.9	5.7	−4.0	6.2	−1.9	4.0
(a)–(c), Small vs. Large	350	−1.1	5.0	7.8	5.5	−6.7**	3.1
(d)–(e), Non-innovators vs. Innovators	526	6.6*	3.7	−8.1**	4.1	1.5	2.4
(e1)–(e2), NTM vs. NTF innovators	166	−13.2*	7.0	17.1**	7.6	−3.9	4.2

Note Figures represent the percentage share of firms where the survey respondent chose a particular answer in response to the following question: "Do you think your R&D organization is taking appropriate risks in R&D projects to achieve its goals?" Firms where the respondent answered with "Do not know" are excluded. ***, **, and * indicate significance at the 1, 5, and 10% levels respectively

obtained by Graham et al. (2021), who asked the same question in their survey of large North American firms and found that 60.2% respondents felt their firm took the "right amount of risk."

We find that the share of firms where the respondent believes the firm takes too much risk is higher for larger firms: the shares for large, medium, and small firms are 12.1%, 10.2%, and 5.4%, respectively, and the difference between large and small firms and that between medium and small firms are both statistically significant. By contrast, the share of firms where respondents felt their firm takes an appropriate level of risk is highest for small firms (73.7%).

The share of firms where respondents felt their firm takes the appropriate level of risk is significantly higher for product innovators (72.0%) than non-innovators (63.9%), suggesting taking the right amount of risk is important for product innovation. Among product innovators, the share of new-to-market innovators where respondents thought their firm takes the appropriate level of risk is 82.4%, which is significantly larger than the corresponding share for new-to-firm innovators (65.2%). In contrast, the share of new-to-market innovators where respondents thought that their firm does not take much risk is 13.7%, which is significantly smaller than the corresponding share for new-to-firm innovators (27.0%). Again, this result suggests that appropriate risk taking is important for explorative innovations.

Table 1.26 shows the results for the following question: "Suppose there is an R&D project that is expected to generate gross sales of 100 million yen immediately if it is successful but gross sales of 0 yen if it fails. Assume that the probability that the project is successful is 10%. How much would you invest in the project?" This question also tries to capture firms' subjective risk preferences, again based on respondents' own judgement. The expected return of this R&D project is 10 million yen ($10\% \times 100$ million yen), meaning that a risk-neutral firm would invest 10 million yen.[24] Accordingly, in Table 1.26, we classify firms as "risk-neutral" if they are willing to invest 10 million yen, as "risk-averse" if they are willing to invest less than 10 million yen, and as "risk-tolerant" if they are willing to invest more than 10 million yen.

We find that the share of risk-averse firms is 37.4%, that of risk-neutral firms 30.8%, and that of risk-tolerant firms 31.8%. The t-tests among the subsamples indicate that there are no significant differences in these shares among small, medium, and large firms; between product innovators and non-innovators; and between new-to-market and new-to-firm innovators.

Finally, in the survey we asked a hypothetical question about the choice between two otherwise identical R&D projects. Project 1 offers a larger expected cumulative profit (net present value) but is expected to make losses for several years after the launch of the product. Project 2 has a smaller expected cumulative profit (net present value) but is expected to generate stable profits after the launch of the product. We assume all other conditions (e.g., initial investment costs, the probability of success of the project, project duration, etc.) are the same for both Projects 1 and 2. We expect

---

[24] We assume that respondents did not consider the costs involved in making the product when answering this question.

1.8 Risk Preferences and Corporate Culture

Table 1.26 Risk preferences: Risk aversion

	N	Risk-averse		Risk-neutral		Risk-tolerant	
		Share (%)	S.D.	Share (%)	S.D.	Share (%)	S.D.
Entire sample	588	37.4	48.4	30.8	46.2	31.8	46.6
By firm size							
(a) Small	306	39.9	49.0	30.7	46.2	29.4	45.6
(b) Medium	190	33.7	47.4	31.1	46.4	35.3	47.9
(c) Large	92	37.0	48.5	30.4	46.3	32.6	47.1
Non-innovators vs. Innovators							
(d) Non-innovators	269	36.4	48.2	30.5	46.1	33.1	47.1
(e) Innovators	319	38.2	48.7	31.0	46.3	30.7	46.2
New-to-market vs. New-to-firm innovators							
(e1) New-to-market (NTM) innovators	57	43.9	50.1	24.6	43.4	31.6	46.9
(e2) New-to-firm (NTF) innovators	132	39.4	49.0	32.6	47.0	28.0	45.1
Difference	N	Share (%)	S.E.	Share (%)	S.E.	Share (%)	S.E.
(a)–(b), Small vs. Medium	496	6.2	4.5	−0.3	4.3	−5.9	4.3
(b)–(c), Medium vs. Large	282	−3.3	6.1	0.6	5.9	2.7	6.1
(a)–(c), Small vs. Large	398	2.9	5.8	0.3	5.5	−3.2	5.5
(d)–(e), Non-innovators vs. Innovators	588	−1.8	4.0	−0.6	3.8	2.4	3.9
(e1)–(e2), NTM vs. NTF innovators	189	4.5	7.8	−8.0	7.3	3.5	7.2

Note This table is constructed using responses to the following question: "Suppose there is an R&D project that is expected to generate gross sales of 100 million yen immediately if it is successful but gross sales of 0 yen if it fails. Assume that the probability that the project is successful is 10% (hence, the probability of failure is 90%). How much would you invest in the project? Please enter the approximate amount." Firms are classified as "risk-neutral" if the investment amount is 10 million yen, as "risk-averse" if the investment amount is less than 10 million yen, and as "risk-tolerant" if the investment amount exceeds 10 million yen. ***, **, and * indicate significance at the 1, 5, and 10% levels respectively

that less risk-averse firm will choose Project 1 and more risk-averse firms will choose Project 2. Graham et al. (2021) ask a similar question in their corporate survey and argue that this question also measures the short-termism of a firm. In this regard, we expect firms that have a larger discount factor to choose the NPV-inferior Project 2 and firms that tolerate early losses to choose the NPV-superior Project 1.

Table 1.27 presents the result. Among the 606 firms that responded to this question, 174 firms (27.7%) replied with "do not know." We exclude these firms, leaving us with 432 observations. Table 1.27 shows that 28.7% of firms would choose Project 1 and the remaining 71.3% would choose Project 2. Graham et al. (2021) report that 59.4% of the firms responding to their survey chose Project 1, which is completely different from our result. The result of our survey suggests that many Japanese firms tend to avoid short-term losses even if a project makes a long-term profit, which

Table 1.27 Risk preferences: Choice regarding an NPV-superior but initially unprofitable project

	N	Share (%)	S.D.
Entire sample	432	28.7	45.3
By firm size			
(a) Small	225	22.7	42.0
(b) Medium	141	32.6	47.1
(c) Large	66	40.9	49.5
Non-innovators vs. Innovators			
(d) Non-innovators	182	23.6	42.6
(e) Innovators	250	32.4	46.9
New-to-market vs. New-to-firm innovators			
(e1) New-to-market (NTM) innovators	38	42.1	50.0
(e2) New-to-firm (NTF) innovators	107	27.1	44.7
Difference	N	Share (%)	S.E.
(a)–(b), Small vs. Medium	366	−10.0**	4.7
(b)–(c), Medium vs. Large	207	−8.3	7.1
(a)–(c), Small vs. Large	291	−18.2***	6.1
(d)–(e), Non-innovators vs. Innovators	432	−8.8**	4.4
(e1)–(e2), NTM vs. NTF innovators	145	15.0*	8.7

Note This table is constructed using responses to the following question: "Suppose the following two R&D projects: Project 1: The expected cumulative profit (net present value) is large, but the project is expected make losses for several years after the launch of the product. Project 2: The expected cumulative profit (net present value) is small, but the project is expected to generate stable profits after the launch of the product. Assume all other conditions (e.g., initial investment costs, the probability of success of the project, project duration, etc.) are the same for both Projects 1 and 2. Which project would you choose?" The table shows the share of firms that chose Project 1. ***, **, and * indicate significance at the 1, 5, and 10% levels respectively

suggests that Japanese firms are more risk-averse or more myopic than U.S. firms regarding the choice of R&D projects.

Next, comparing subsamples, we find that larger firms are more likely to choose the NPV-superior Project 1: the share of firms that would choose Project 1 is 40.9% among large firms, 32.6% among medium firms, and 22.7% among small firms, and the differences between large and small firms and between medium and small firms are both significant. While this suggests that larger firms are more risk-tolerant, it should be noted that there may be other factors that affect firms' choice. For example, small firms are more likely to be financially constrained, and this might make them choose Project 2, which generates a stable cash flow after the launch of the product. In this case, small firms are not necessarily inherently more risk averse; instead, their choice might reflect financial constraints, and if such constraints were controlled for, their risk aversion may not differ from larger firms.

Further, we find that product innovators (32.4%) are more likely to choose Project 1 than non-innovators (23.6%). This suggests that firms that succeeded in making product innovations are more risk tolerant. Among innovating firms, we find that the share of new-to-market innovators (42.1%) that would choose Project 1 is significantly larger than that of new-to-firm innovators (27.1%), indicating that new-to-market innovators are more risk tolerant and/or more tolerant of early losses than new-to-firm innovators.

To sum up, the results for our first question about risk preferences suggest that taking the appropriate level of risk is important for product innovation, especially for new-to-market innovation. The results for the second question about risk preferences are similar for product innovators and non-innovators and for new-to-market and new-to-firm innovators, suggesting that there is no link between risk preferences and innovation. The results for our third question regarding risk preferences indicate that product innovators, especially new-to-market innovators, are more risk tolerant and immune to short-termism. The results for the first and third questions are consistent with studies reporting a positive effect of risk tolerance on innovation and/or exploration (Ederer and Manso 2013; Krieger et al. 2022; Carson et al. 2020; Tian and Wang 2014). It should be noted, however, that how risk preferences are linked with innovation depends on the empirical proxy used for risk preferences.

1.8.2 Corporate Culture

To measure a firm's corporate culture in the Competing Values Framework (CVF) developed by Cameron et al. (2014) (see Sect. 1.2.4), we asked firms to choose up to three options out of eight to describe their corporate culture. The eight options that we provided were "teamwork," "bottom-up approach," "leadership," "rule-based decision making," "customer first," "profitability," "market impact," and "creativity." We chose these options based on studies employing the CVF (Cameron et al. 2014;

Fiordelisi and Ricci 2014; Thakor 2016; Hanaeda et al. 2020). The options correspond to the following quadrants: "teamwork" and "bottom-up approach" represent a *Collaborate*-oriented culture, "leadership" and "rule-based decision making" represent a *Control*-oriented culture, "customer first" and "profitability" represent a *Compete*-oriented culture, and "market impact" and "creativity" represent a *Create*-oriented culture.

Table 1.28 shows the percentage shares of firms that chose each option. Note that these shares do not add up to 100 percent because firms were asked to choose up to three options. The option that firms chose most frequently is "customer first" (72.4%), followed by "profitability" (45.0%), "teamwork" (36.0%), and "creativity" (29.9%). Because the top two options, "customer first" and "profitability," represent a *Compete*-oriented culture, it appears that many Japanese firms value competitiveness and prioritize customers and shareholders.

Significantly larger shares of large firms than small and/or medium firms chose "bottom-up approach," "rule-based decision making," and "customer first." On the other hand, significantly larger shares of small firms than medium and/or large firms chose "market impact" and "creativity," both of which correspond to a *Create*-oriented culture. The latter result suggests that many small firms value creativity.

We fail to find any correlations between corporate culture, including a *Create*-oriented culture, and the likelihood of making product innovations. The difference in the percentage shares of each of the options between product innovators and non-innovators are all insignificant. We find, however, a significant difference between new-to-market innovators and new-to-firm innovators: the share of new-to-market innovators that chose "market impact" (29.8%) and "creativity" (43.9%) is significantly larger than that of new-to-firm innovators (market impact: 12.5%, creativity: 18.4%). This indicates that, among firms that succeeded in making product innovations, new-to-market innovators put high value on creativity as part of their corporate culture.

As discussed in Sect. 1.2.4, as far as we are aware, there are no empirical studies that examine the relationship between corporate culture and innovation using the CVF. We note, however, that our finding that new-to-market innovation is positively associated with a *Create*-oriented culture is consistent, or at least not inconsistent, with the study by Graham et al. (2021), who do not use the CVF but find that "adaptability," which is one of the cultural values they measure, is positively correlated with creativity. Because "adaptability" corresponds to an orientation toward "individuality and flexibility" in the CVF (on the top of the Y axis in Fig. 1.1), firms with a culture that values adaptability can be classified as falling into either the *Collaborate* or *Create* quadrants. In addition, the finding that new-to-market innovators put higher value on creativity than new-to-firm innovators is consistent with Manso's (2011) theoretical conjecture that a corporate culture that tolerates early failure and rewards long-term success motivates exploration.

1.8 Risk Preferences and Corporate Culture

Table 1.28 Corporate culture using the CVF

	N	Collaborate-oriented						Control-oriented					
		Teamwork		Bottom-up approach				Leadership				Rule-based decision making	
		Share (%)	S.D.	Share (%)	S.D.			Share (%)	S.D.			Share (%)	S.D.
Entire sample	609	36.0	48.0	8.9	28.5			12.6	33.3			20.2	40.2
By firm size													
(a) Small	313	34.8	47.7	6.7	25.1			13.7	34.5			16.3	37.0
(b) Medium	195	35.9	48.1	9.2	29.0			12.3	32.9			23.1	42.2
(c) Large	101	39.6	49.2	14.9	35.7			9.9	30.0			26.7	44.5
Non-innovators vs. Innovators													
(d) Non-innovators	277	35.4	47.9	6.9	25.3			12.6	33.3			17.7	38.2
(e) Innovators	330	36.4	48.2	10.6	30.8			12.4	33.0			22.4	41.8
New-to-market vs. New-to-firm innovators													
(e1) New-to-market (NTM) innovators	57	29.8	46.2	5.3	22.5			8.8	28.5			21.1	41.1
(e2) New-to-firm (NTF) innovators	136	39.7	49.1	13.2	34.0			13.2	34.0			25.0	43.5
Difference	N	Share (%)	S.E.	Share (%)	S.E.			Share (%)	S.E.			Share (%)	S.E.
(a)–(b), Small vs. Medium	508	−1.1	4.4	−2.5	2.4			1.4	3.1			−6.8*	3.6
(b)–(c), Medium vs. Large	296	−3.7	5.9	−5.6	3.9			2.4	3.9			−3.7	5.3
(a)–(c), Small vs. Large	414	−4.8	5.5	−8.1**	3.2			3.8	3.8			−10.4**	4.5
(d)–(e), Non-innovators vs. Innovators	607	−1.0	3.9	−3.7	2.3			0.2	2.7			−4.7	3.3
(e1)–(e2), NTM vs. NTF innovators	193	−9.9	7.6	−8.0	4.9			−4.5	5.1			−3.9	6.8

(continued)

Table 1.28 Corporate culture using the CVF

	N	Compete-oriented				Create-oriented					
		Customer first		Profitability		Market impact		Creativity			
		Share (%)	S.D.	Share (%)	S.D.	Share (%)	S.D.	Share (%)	S.D.		
Entire sample	609	72.4	44.7	45.0	49.8	16.6	37.2	29.9	45.8		
By firm size											
(a) Small	313	69.0	46.3	45.4	49.9	19.5	39.7	35.8	48.0		
(b) Medium	195	73.3	44.3	47.2	50.0	14.9	35.7	23.1	42.2		
(c) Large	101	81.2	39.3	39.6	49.2	10.9	31.3	24.8	43.4		
Non-innovators vs. Innovators											
(d) Non-innovators	277	70.4	45.7	46.9	50.0	15.5	36.3	30.0	45.9		
(e) Innovators	330	74.2	43.8	43.3	49.6	17.6	38.1	29.4	45.6		
New-to-market vs. New-to-firm innovators											
(e1) New-to-market (NTM) innovators	57	68.4	46.9	42.1	49.8	29.8	46.2	43.9	50.1		
(e2) New-to-firm (NTF) innovators	136	73.5	44.3	39.7	49.1	12.5	33.2	18.4	38.9		
Difference	N	Share (%)	S.E.	Share (%)	S.E.	Share (%)	S.E.	Share (%)	S.E.		
(a)–(b), Small vs. Medium	508	−4.3	4.2	−1.8	4.6	4.6	3.5	12.7***	4.2		
(b)–(c), Medium vs. Large	296	−7.9	5.2	7.6	6.1	4.0	4.2	−1.7	5.2		
(a)–(c), Small vs. Large	414	−12.2**	5.1	5.8	5.7	8.6**	4.3	11.0**	5.4		
(d)–(e), Non-innovators vs. Innovators	607	−3.8	3.6	3.6	4.1	−2.1	3.0	0.6	3.7		
(e1)–(e2), NTM vs. NTF innovators	193	−5.1	7.1	2.4	7.8	17.3***	5.9	25.5***	6.7		

Note Respondent firms were asked to choose up to three options that describe the firm's corporate culture. ***, **, and * indicate significance at the 1, 5, and 10% levels respectively

1.9 Conclusion

This monograph provided a detailed account of the current R&D management practices in Japanese firms based on a unique firm survey. Using data from the survey, we presented descriptive statistics and conducted t-tests to make inferences about the link between R&D management practices and (i) firms' success in making product innovation and (ii) the choice between exploration (new-to-market product innovation) and exploitation (new-to-firm product innovation) among product innovators. We find many interesting and instructive facts about the R&D management practices of Japanese firms. Specifically, we find the following.

- *Organizational structure of R&D* (Sect. 1.5): Product innovators are more likely to have a "hybrid" R&D organizational structure with both centralized and decentralized R&D activities than non-innovators. While some studies find that firms with a centralized R&D structure are more likely to generate explorative innovations that have a higher level of impact (e.g., Argyres and Silverman 2004), we do not find a link between new-to-market product innovation and the likelihood of having a centralized R&D structure.

  Regarding the delegation of authority to R&D organizations, we find that the share of firms where both the R&D organization and the human resources department take the initiative in hiring R&D personnel is higher among product innovators than non-innovators. In contrast, the share of firms where the R&D organization takes the initiative is significantly lower for product innovators than non-innovators. These results suggest that there is no link, or a negative link, between the delegation of authority in hiring R&D personnel and the success of product innovation. However, among product innovators, the share of firms where the R&D organization takes the initiative is higher among new-to-market innovators than new-to-firm innovators. This result is consistent with studies finding that the delegation of authority to R&D organizations promotes exploration (Acemoglu et al. 2007; Kastl et al. 2013). We note, however, that in Sect. 1.6.1.3 we do not find a link between new-to-market innovation and the delegation of authority regarding R&D project management. It seems safe to conclude that whether delegation of authority to R&D organizations motivates exploration is ambiguous and depends on the empirical proxy used.

- *Staged project management* (Sect. 1.6): Product innovators are more likely to implement staged project management, set interim goals (milestones), and provide feedback to R&D personnel than non-innovators. Regarding the choice between exploration and exploitation, we find that firms that introduced new-to-market product innovations are more likely to incorporate opinions from external experts into interim feedback. This result is consistent with theoretical studies predicting that timely feedback on performance promotes explorative innovation (Manso 2011) and empirical studies that find a positive link between feedback and exploration (Azoulay et al. 2011). There are no significant differences between product innovators and non-innovators and between new-to-market innovators and new-to-firm innovators regarding the extent to which firms consider the achievement of milestones as important when deciding whether to continue an R&D project. This result suggests that the effect of the threat of termination on innovation, in particular explorative innovation, is ambiguous. Our result is consistent with Manso's (2011) theoretical prediction but inconsistent with empirical findings by Ederer and Manso (2013) and Mao et al. (2014), who find that the threat of termination is detrimental to exploration.

- *Compensation and incentive schemes for R&D personnel* (Sect. 1.7): Product innovators are more likely to employ a salary scheme based on performance-based pay, put greater weight on performance than ability in the evaluation of R&D personnel, and employ pecuniary incentive schemes such as rewards based on the number of patent applications, than non-innovators. We also find that, among product innovators, new-to-market innovators are more likely to employ patent applications/registrations as a criterion in evaluating R&D personnel than new-to-firm innovators. Our results are consistent with studies that find a positive link between innovation and pay-for-performance (e.g., Foss and Laursen 2005). Further, they are also consistent with studies that find a positive link between innovation and pecuniary incentives (Onishi 2013; Sauermann and Cohen 2010) but inconsistent with theoretical studies arguing that pecuniary incentives for R&D employees may adversely affect their intrinsic motivation (Bénabou and Tirole 2003; Kreps 1997) and empirical studies reporting a negative link between innovation and pecuniary incentives (e.g., Onishi et al. 2021). While some studies find a positive link between innovation and non-pecuniary incentives (e.g., Sauermann and Cohen 2010), we do not find such evidence. Finally, we find that the share of firms that employ invention reward schemes, in which R&D employees receive rewards based on the amount of profits the firm has made from the inventions and patents that the R&D employee was engaged in, are larger for product innovators than non-innovators. We also find that product innovators are more likely to have a director on the board who belonged to an R&D organization in the past than non-innovators, which suggests that there is a positive link between innovation and reward for long-term success. However, we do not find any evidence for a positive link between new-to-market innovation and reward for long-term success, which means that we do not find support for Manso's (2011) argument that reward for long-term success encourages exploration.

- *Risk preferences and corporate culture* (Sect. 1.8): Using the three questions that try to capture a firm's risk preferences, we find that product innovators are more likely to take the appropriate level of risk than non-innovators. We also find that product innovators are more risk-tolerant and immune to short-termism. The results that product innovators are taking the appropriate level of risk and are risk-tolerant are driven mainly by new-to-market rather than new-to-firm innovators. Our results are consistent with studies that find a positive link between risk tolerance and innovation and/or exploration (Ederer and Manso 2013; Krieger et al. 2022; Carson et al. 2020; Tian and Wang 2014). We note, however, that how risk preferences are associated with innovation depends on the way risk preferences are measured.

1.9 Conclusion

We find no link between product innovation and any of the corporate cultures (quadrants) identified by the CVF. We find, however, that among product innovators, new-to-market innovators put higher value on a *Create*-oriented culture than new-to-firm innovators, which suggests that corporate culture does play an important role in motivating explorative innovation, as suggested by Manso (2011).

In our discussion of the survey results, we linked the various findings with the theoretical and empirical literature on which our survey questions were based in order to outline possible mechanisms at work. However, the findings based on descriptive statistics and univariate analyses using t-tests represent only a first step, and more rigorous statistical analyses employing multivariate regression models to examine the link between R&D organization and innovation while controlling for a range of factors are needed. Such factors include differences in firm size, industry, and firms' financial condition.

Moreover, there were other findings which we did not investigate much in this monograph. For instance, we found that the empirical link between some of the R&D management practices (such as the delegation of authority to hire employees to R&D organization and the implementation of staged project management) and innovation outcomes depends on the proxy used for innovation outcomes—in our case, whether a firm has made any product innovations or new-to-market product innovations. This suggests that a management practice that is effective in increasing the likelihood of product innovation may not be effective in encouraging explorative innovation. We leave this issue as well as more rigorous analyses for future research.

Open Access This chapter is licensed under the terms of the Creative Commons Attribution 4.0 International License (http://creativecommons.org/licenses/by/4.0/), which permits use, sharing, adaptation, distribution and reproduction in any medium or format, as long as you give appropriate credit to the original author(s) and the source, provide a link to the Creative Commons license and indicate if changes were made.

The images or other third party material in this chapter are included in the chapter's Creative Commons license, unless indicated otherwise in a credit line to the material. If material is not included in the chapter's Creative Commons license and your intended use is not permitted by statutory regulation or exceeds the permitted use, you will need to obtain permission directly from the copyright holder.

Appendix

Survey of R&D Management Practices

- This survey is supported by Grants-in-Aid for Scientific Research (B) provided by the Japan Society for the Promotion of Science.
- Your responses are strictly confidential and no information provided by individual survey participants will be disclosed. Survey results will be statistically processed maintaining anonymity.
- We recommend that you respond online. Access the following URL (https://research.surece.co.jp/rd-mgmt2020/) and log in using the ID and password provided in the attached "Request for online response."
- Please submit the completed questionnaire by **February 17, 2020** (**Monday**).
- We will send a summary report of the survey results to survey participants that have responded.
- Unless otherwise stated, provide your answers as of FY2018.
- Answer all questions on a non-consolidated basis, that is, on the basis of the activities of your company only and exclude those of affiliated companies including the parent company and subsidiaries.
- For a definition of "R&D" in this survey and detailed definitions of terms marked with * in the questionnaire, see the glossary of terms attached to this survey.
- In what follows, we will ask about (1) R&D expenditure, R&D personnel, and R&D organizational structure, (2) R&D project management, (3) personnel evaluation of researchers and engineers, and (4) R&D outputs. We would appreciate it if the person most qualified to respond to these issues answers the survey.

1. R&D expenditure, R&D personnel, and R&D organizational structure

These questions are about the R&D expenditure*[1] of your company.

Q1: Please provide the approximate percentage shares of funding sources for R&D expenditure.

Funding from headquarters (or the business unit to which R&D organization belongs)	Commissions received from other business units within the company	Funding from outside the company (commissions, subsidies, grants, etc.)	Other	Total
%	%	%	%	100%

*[1] "R&D expenditure" refers to the total amount of R&D expenditure spent inside and outside the company, irrespective of the source of the funds (your own funds, externally received funds, etc.).

Q2: To what extent do you take the following items (a)-(f) into account when determining total R&D expenditure? Choose <u>one</u> answer for each item.

	Fully taken into account	To some extent taken into account	Not very much taken into account	Not taken into account at all
(a) Gross sales in the previous year	○	○	○	○
(b) Profits in the previous year	○	○	○	○
(c) R&D expenditure in the previous year	○	○	○	○
(d) Labor costs of R&D organization(s)	○	○	○	○
(e) Cumulative costs of individual R&D projects	○	○	○	○
(f) Annual sales goals for new products as a share of total sales	○	○	○	○

Appendix

The following questions are about your company's R&D personnel. *2

Q3: Please provide the approximate age composition of your R&D personnel (percentage shares).

Under 24 y/o	From 25 to 34 y/o	From 35 to 44 y/o	From 45 to 54 y/o	55 y/o and older	Total
%	%	%	%	%	100%

*2) "R&D personnel" refers to persons who have at least a bachelor's degree (excluding junior college) or have equivalent or greater expertise, conduct R&D activities on their own specific topic, and engage in R&D activities for more than half of their working hours.

Q4: Which department takes the initiative in hiring R&D personnel? Choose one answer.

○ R&D organization takes the initiative	○ Human resources department takes the initiative	○ Both R&D organization and human resources department take the initiative	○ Other

Q5: To what extent are researchers' own wishes taken into account when transferring R&D personnel? Choose one answer.

○ Fully taken into account	○ To some extent taken into account	○ Not very much taken into account	○ Not taken into account at all

The following questions are about your R&D organization(s). *3

Q6: How many R&D organizations does your company have?

Number of R&D organizations	
	(Number of R&D organizations overseas)

*3) "R&D organization" refers to an organization (e.g., department, division) in which R&D personnel mainly conduct R&D. Even if the name of the organization does not include "research" or "development," an organization that conducts R&D activities is regarded as an "R&D organization" for the purpose of this survey. Please provide the number of organizations that in your company's organization chart can be regarded as "R&D organizations."

Q7: Among the R&D organizations in Q6, does your company have one or more R&D organizations that are (a) highly independent of business units and/or (b) directly controlled by business units? Choose all that apply.

☐	(a) My company has one or more R&D organizations that are highly independent of business units (e.g., central research laboratory, development department).
☐	(b) My company has one or more R&D organizations that are directly controlled by business units (e.g., pharmaceuticals development division).

Only answer Q8 to Q10 if you chose both (a) and (b) in Q7; otherwise, proceed to Q11.

Q8: Specify the number of R&D organizations falling under (a) and (b) in Q7, respectively.

(a) R&D organizations that are highly independent of business units	(b) R&D organizations that are directly controlled by business units

Q9: Please provide the approximate R&D expenditure shares of R&D organizations falling under (a) and (b) in Q7, respectively.

(a) R&D organizations that are highly independent of business units	(b) R&D organizations that are directly controlled by business units	Total
%	%	100%

Q10: Please provide the approximate shares of R&D personnel belonging to R&D organizations falling under (a) and (b) in Q7, respectively.

(a) R&D organizations that are highly independent of business units	(b) R&D organizations that are directly controlled by business units	Total
%	%	100%

2. R&D project management

The following questions are about the number of R&D projects. [*4]

Q11: Please specify the approximate number of R&D projects in progress.

Number of R&D projects in progress	Projects

*4) "R&D project" refers to R&D activities for which the R&D personnel involved, a budget, a deadline, etc., have been set in order to achieve specific research outcomes.

Q12: Please provide the approximate share of R&D projects that have continuously been ongoing for more than three years.

Percentage of R&D projects that have continuously been ongoing for more than three years	%

Appendix

Q13: Do you have any R&D projects that have been terminated or suspended within the past three years? Choose <u>one</u> answer.

○ Yes   ○ No

Q14: Please provide the approximate share of projects where R&D organizations have the authority to decide whether to terminate/suspend or continue the project. Moreover, if there is a pre-determined upper limit to the R&D expenditure up to which R&D organizations have the authority to decide whether to terminate/suspend or continue the project, please check "Pre-determined" and enter the approximate amount.

Percentage of projects where the R&D organization has the authority to decide to terminate/suspend or continue the project	Upper limit to R&D expenditure up to which R&D organization has authority to decide whether to terminate/suspend or continue the project. If there is a pre-determined limit, please enter the approximate amount.
☐☐☐ %	Pre-determined ○⇒ ☐☐☐☐ million yen Not pre-determined ○

The following questions are about your R&D project management.

Q15: Please specify the average number of years from the commencement of an R&D project to the achievement of final results.

Average number of years from the commencement of an R&D project to the achievement of final results	Year(s)

Q16: Do you implement staged project management*⁵ for your R&D projects? Choose <u>one</u> answer. If you do, specify the average number of stages.

Yes ○⇒	Number of stages
No ○⇒ Proceed to Q21	

*5) "Staged project management" refers to a method of R&D project management in which the project proceeds in consecutive multiple stages (phases). Staged project management is accompanied by an interim evaluation, which determines whether the project should be terminated/suspended/continued and reviews the project schedule.

Only answer Q17 if you chose "Yes" in Q16; otherwise, proceed to Q21.

Q17: Do you set intermediate goals ("milestones") for the interim evaluation of projects? Choose <u>one</u> answer.

Yes ○
No ○ ⇒ proceed to Q19

Only answer Q18 if you chose "Yes" in Q17; otherwise, proceed to Q19.

Q18: To what extent do you take into account whether intermediate goals (milestones) were achieved when assessing whether to terminate/suspend or continue the R&D project? Choose one answer for (a) initial stages and (b) late stages, respectively.

Whether intermediate goals were achieved	Fully taken into account	To some extent taken into account	Not very much taken into account	Not taken into account at all
(a) Initial stages (e.g., idea/basic research)	○	○	○	○
(b) Late stages (e.g., preparation for launching new goods/services)	○	○	○	○

Only answer Q19 if you chose "Yes" in Q16; otherwise, proceed to Q21.

Q19: Do you provide feedback on the interim evaluation results to the R&D personnel in charge of the project? Choose one answer.

Yes ○
No ○ ⇒ proceed to Q19

Only answer Q20 if you chose "Yes" in Q19; otherwise, proceed to Q21.

Q20: Do you incorporate the following items (a)–(c) when providing feedback on the interim evaluation results? Choose all applicable answers for each item. If you do not incorporate them, choose "Not incorporated."

	Initial stages (e.g., ideas/basic research)	Late stages (e.g., preparation for launching new goods/services)	Not incorporated
(a) Opinions from other research teams in the same or other R&D organizations	☐	☐	☐
(b) Opinions from non-R&D organizations (business units and head office) within your company	☐	☐	☐
(c) Opinions (including informal ones) from external experts outside your company	☐	☐	☐

The following questions are about your company's preferences with regard to R&D projects and corporate culture.

Note: Please answer Q21–Q24 based on your own judgement.

Q21: Suppose there is an R&D project that is expected to generate gross sales of 100 million yen immediately if it is successful but gross sales of 0 yen if it fails. Assume that the probability that the project is successful is 10% (hence, the probability of failure is 90%). How much would you invest in the project? Please enter the approximate amount.

[____] million yen

Appendix

Q22: Suppose the following two R&D projects:
- Project 1: The expected cumulative profit (net present value) is large, but the project is expected make losses for several years after the launch of the product.
- Project 2: The expected cumulative profit (net present value) is small, but the project is expected to generate stable profits after the launch of the product.

Assume all other conditions (e.g., initial investment costs, the probability of success of the project, project duration, etc.) are the same for both Projects 1 and 2.
Which project do you think your company would choose? Choose one answer.

○ Project 1   ○ Project 2   ○ Do not know

Q23: Do you think your R&D organization is taking appropriate risks in R&D projects to achieve its goals? Choose one answer.

○ Does not take much risk   ○ Takes appropriate level of risk   ○ Takes too much risk   ○ Do not know

Q24: Choose up to three words that describe your company's corporate culture.

☐ (a) Teamwork	☐ (b) Leadership	☐ (c) Customer first	☐ (d) Market impact
☐ (e) Creativity	☐ (f) Profitability	☐ (g) Rule-based decision making	☐ (h) Bottom-up approach
☐ (i) Other (			)

3. Evaluation of R&D personnel

The following questions are about the evaluation of R&D personnel in your company.

Q25: What salary scheme do you employ for R&D personnel? Choose all that apply.

☐	[a] A specific salary scheme for R&D personnel that differs from that for other employees	☐	[b] Starting salary varies depending on the educational background
☐	[c] Salary scheme based on performance-based pay	☐	[d] R&D personnel can choose from among various salary schemes
☐	[e] None of the salary schemes from [a]–[d] is employed.		

Q26: Assume an R&D employee in their early 30s is being evaluated. Approximately what weights would be put on their ability and their performance in their evaluation?[*6]

Ability	Performance	Total
☐☐☐ %	☐☐☐ %	100%

*6) "Ability" refers to the abilities demonstrated in performing the job. "Performance" refers to the level of achievement met in performing the job.

Q27: Do you employ the following criteria for the evaluation of R&D personnel? Choose all that apply.

☐ [a] Research papers and conference presentations	☐ [b] Patent applications/registrations	☐ [c] Commercialization (Launch) of new products
☐ [d] Amount of sales generated by new products to which the R&D employee contributed	☐ [e] R&D progress, including compliance with schedule	☐ [f] Acquisition of qualifications/degrees
☐ [g] None of the criteria from [a]–[f] are employed		

Q28: Do you employ the following incentive schemes for R&D personnel? Choose all items that apply.

☐ [a] In-house research presentations	☐ [b] Dispatch to university and/or support for studying abroad	☐ [c] Open recruitment for R&D projects
☐ [d] Awards for outstanding R&D results	☐ [e] Rewards based on the number of patent applications	☐ [f] Rewards based on the amount of profits from inventions and patents (invention reward schemes)
☐ [g] None of the schemes from [a]–[f] are employed		

Q29: Did any of the directors on the board (e.g., chairperson, president, vice president) belong to an R&D organization in the past? Choose one answer.

◯ Yes   ◯ No

4. R&D results

The following questions are about the R&D results of your company.

Q30: Did you make process innovations (introduce new or improved production processes and/or delivery methods, etc.)[*7] during the three years from FY2016 to FY2018? Choose one answer.

◯ Yes   ◯ No

Appendix

Q31: Did you make product innovations (introduce new or improved goods or services in the market)*[8] during the three years from FY2016 to FY2018? Choose one answer.

○ Yes   ○ No

Only answer Q32 if you chose "Yes" in Q31. Q32 concerns the novelty of, and turnover (revenue) from product innovations introduced in the market.

Q32: Did you introduce the following types of product innovations in the market from FY2016 to FY2018? Choose all types of product innovations that apply and provide the percentage of total sales that such product innovations generated in FY2018. Also specify the approximate sales share of all products other than (X) and (Y) in FY2018.

	Introduced product innovations in the market (Over the 3 years from FY2016 to FY2018)	Percentage of total sales in FY2018
(X) New or significantly improved goods/services that no competitor was offering (new goods and services in the market)	☐	___ %
(Y) New or improved goods/services that were almost the same as or very similar to ones already offered by competitors (new goods and services for your company only)	☐	___ %
(Z) All other goods/services other than (X) and (Y) above (including goods/services that remained unchanged or were only marginally modified and the resale of products purchased from other companies)	(Z) = 100 − [(X) + (Y)]	___ %
Total sales in FY2018	(X) + (Y) + (Z)	1 0 0 %

This is the end of the questions. Please write about yourself.
(This information will be used for sending you the survey results and for inquiries regarding your responses, if any.)

Name		Department		Job title	
Number of years with the company	○ No more than 5 years ○ From 6 to 10 years ○ From 11 to 15 years ○ From 16 to 20 years ○ More than 21 years					
Telephone number			E-mail address		

Thank you for participating in our survey.

Glossary of Terms in the "Survey of R&D Management Practices"

Research and Development
"Research and development (R&D)" refers to systematic research and creative efforts in science and technology undertaken for the acquisition of new knowledge on materials, functions, and natural phenomena, and for new applications of the existing store of knowledge. R&D includes not only academic research but also activities related to the development of new products, the improvement of existing products, and the development and technical improvement of products or production processes. For the purpose of this survey, R&D does not include activities for sales or management-related purposes.

*1) R&D Expenditure
The term "R&D expenditure" refers to the total amount of expenses on R&D, irrespective of whether such expenses are funded internally (e.g., through retained earnings) or externally (e.g., through grants from the government). R&D expenditure includes expenditures spent within and outside your company. R&D expenditure spent within your company includes labor costs; expenditures on raw materials, tangible fixed assets, intangible fixed assets, and consumable supplies such as books; lease fees, etc. R&D expenditure spent outside your company refers to payments to outside vendors, irrespective of whether such payments are in the form of money in trust, subsides, allocations, etc.

*2) R&D Personnel
"R&D personnel" refers to individuals holding at least a bachelor's degree (or having equivalent or greater expertise) and engaged in R&D activities in their area of expertise for more than half of their working hours. For the purpose of this survey, "R&D personnel" does not include the following persons: persons who mainly assist R&D personnel, persons who are engaged in technical services related to R&D activities under the guidance and supervision of R&D personnel, and persons who are engaged in clerical work, administration, accounting, etc.

*3) R&D Organizations
The term "R&D organizations" refers to organizations in which R&D personnel mainly conduct R&D. For the purpose of this survey, organizations that perform R&D activities are regarded as "R&D organizations" even if their name does not include the words "Research" or "Development."

For the number of R&D organizations in Q6, please answer with the number of R&D organizations in your company's organization chart. For example, given the organization chart below, the company has *four* R&D organizations, which are boxed in bold. They consist of *three* R&D organizations that are highly independent of business units (i.e., the Development Department, the Central Research Laboratory, and the North American Research Laboratory under the "R&D Unit") corresponding

Appendix

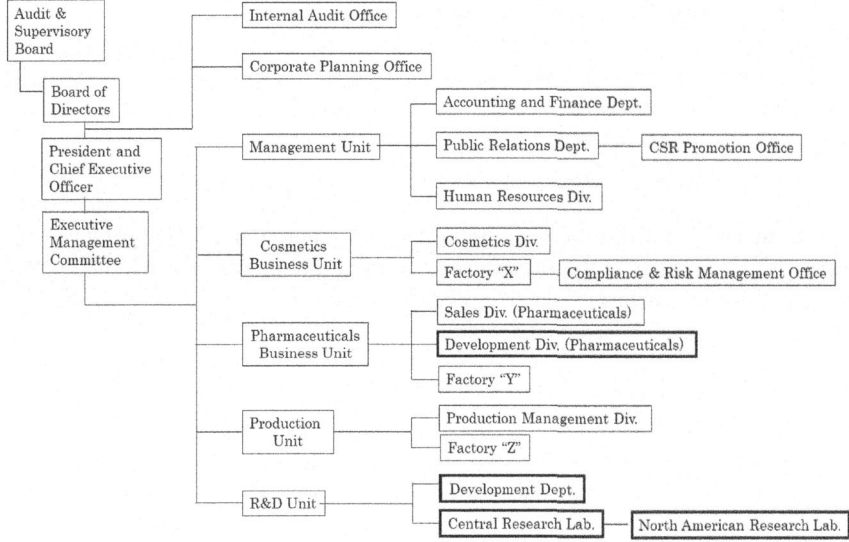

Fig. 1 Example organization chart

to Q7(a) and *one* R&D organization that is directly controlled by a business unit (i.e., the Pharmaceuticals Development Division under the "Pharmaceuticals Business Unit") corresponding to Q7(b).

Please do not include other R&D entities that are not listed in your company's organization chart. For example, the hypothetical company in Fig. 1 also has a cosmetics development section/team under the "Cosmetics Division," but the section/team is not shown in the company organization chart and therefore is not counted as an R&D organization.

*4) R&D Projects

The term "R&D projects" refers to projects that are conducted to accomplish specific research outcomes by a pre-determined deadline and with a designated budget and R&D personnel. Specific research outcomes include not only commercialized goods/services such as "low-power superconducting network devices" but also the development and improvement of production processes such as "an efficiency improvement in the manufacturing process by x%."

*5) Staged Project Management

"Staged project management" refers to the management of R&D projects in consecutive stages, such as "ideation and concept development," "preliminary assessment of commercialization," "development," "testing and validation," and "production and marketing." Staged project management also entails a phase-based interim evaluation that affects the decision about whether the project is continued, suspended, or abandoned, as well as a revision of the schedule.

*6) Ability and Performance in Employee Evaluation
"Ability" in the evaluation of R&D employees refers to a person's potential ability to perform their duties during the evaluation period. This includes "willingness and attitude (e.g., cooperativeness, discipline)," "cognitive ability (e.g., ability to assess and plan)," and "interpersonal skills (e.g., leadership, ability to arbitrate)."

"Performance" in the evaluation of R&D employees refers to a person's results achieved in performing their duties during the evaluation period. Usually, the results to be evaluated are set at the beginning of the evaluation period as "achievement goals," taking account of the importance and difficulty of the person's duties. For example, the results to be evaluated for R&D personnel include "patent applications," "prototype products," "commercialization," etc.

*7) Process Innovation
"Process innovation" refers to new or significantly improved production processes, methods of providing services and of delivering products or support activities. This includes significant improvements in techniques, equipment, and/or software.

Process innovation is defined in this survey as something new to your company; your company does not have to be the first to introduce this process. It does not matter whether the innovation was developed by your company or by other companies.

*8) Product Innovation
"Product innovation" refers to new or significantly improved goods or services with respect to their technical specifications, components and materials, software in the product, user friendliness, or other functional characteristics. This includes new combinations of existing technologies or technology upgrades of existing goods or services. Changes only in aesthetic characteristics or the resale of products invented and/or produced by other companies are not included.

Product innovation in this survey is defined as something new to your company; the good or service does not have to be new to the market. It does not matter whether your company or other companies developed the product innovation.

References

Acemoglu D, Aghion P, Lelarge C, Van Reenen J, Zilibotti F (2007) Technology, information, and the decentralization of the firm. Quart J Econ 122(4):1759–1799
Aghion P, Tirole J (1994) The management of innovation. Quart J Econ 109(4):1185–1209
Aghion P, Tirole J (1997) Formal and real authority in organizations. J Polit Econ 105(1):1–29
Andries P, Hünermund P (2020). Firm-level effects of staged investments in innovation: the moderating role of resource availability. Res Policy 49(7):103994
Argyres NS, Silverman BS (2004) R&D, organization structure, and the development of corporate technological knowledge. Strateg Manag J 25(8–9):929–958
Argyres N, Rios L, Silverman BS (2020) Organizational change and the dynamics of innovation: formal R&D structure and intrafirm inventor networks. Strateg Manag J 41(11):2015–2049
Arora A, Belenzon S, Rios L (2011) The organization of R&D in American corporations: the determinants and consequences of decentralization. NBER Working Paper No. 17013
Arora A, Belenzon S, Rios L (2014) Make, buy, organize: the interplay between research, external knowledge, and firm structure. Strateg Manag J 35(3):317–337
Azoulay P, Zivin JS, Manso G (2011) Incentives and creativity: evidence from the academic life sciences. RAND J Econ 42(3):527–554
Azoulay P, Lerner J (2012) Technological innovation and organizations. In: Gibbons R, Roberts J (eds) The handbook of organizational economics. Princeton, NJ: Princeton University Press.
Bénabou R, Tirole J (2003) Intrinsic and extrinsic motivation. Rev Econ Stud 70(3):489–520
Bloom N, Van Reenen J (2007) Measuring and explaining management practices across firms and countries. Quart J Econ 122(4):1351–1408
Bloom N, Van Reenen J (2010) Why do management practices differ across firms and countries? J Econ Perspect 24(1):203–224
Bloom N, Brynjolfsson E, Foster L, Jarmin R, Patnaik M, Saporta-Ekstein I, Van Reenen J (2019) What drives differences in management practices? Am Econ Rev 109(5):1648–1683
Cameron KS, Quinn RE, DeGraff J, Thakor AV (2014) Competing values leadership, 2nd edn. Edward Elgar Publishing, Cheltenham, UK
Carson R, Graff Zivin JS, Louviere J, Sadoff S, Shrader Jr JG (2020) The risk of caution: evidence from an R&D experiment. NBER Working Paper No. 26847
Cooper RG (1988) The new product process: a decision guide for management. J Mark Manag 3(3):238–255
Cooper RG (2017) Winning at new products: creating value through innovation, 5th edn. Basic Books, New York

Cornelli F, Yosha O (2003) Stage financing and the role of convertible securities. Rev Econ Stud 70(1):1–32
Cramer JS, Hartog J, Jonker N, Van Praag CM (2002) Low risk aversion encourages the choice for entrepreneurship: an empirical test of a truism. J Econ Behav Organ 48(1):29–36
Dahiya S, Ray K (2012) Staged investments in entrepreneurial financing. J Corp Finan 18(5):1193–1216
Dewett T (2007) Linking intrinsic motivation, risk taking, and employee creativity in an R&D environment. R&D Manag 37(3):197–208
Ederer F, Manso G (2013) Is pay for performance detrimental to innovation? Manage Sci 59(7):1496–1513
Fiordelisi F, Ricci O (2014) Corporate culture and CEO turnover. J Corp Finan 28:66–82
Foss NJ, Laursen K (2005) Performance pay, delegation and multitasking under uncertainty and innovativeness: an empirical investigation. J Econ Behav Organ 58(2):246–276
Gibbons R, Roberts J (eds) (2012) The handbook of organizational economics. Princeton University Press, Princeton, NJ
Gompers PA (1995) Optimal investment, monitoring, and the staging of venture capital. Journal of Finance 50(5):1461–1489
Gompers PA, Gornall W, Kaplan SN, Strebulaev IA (2020) How do venture capitalists make decisions? J Financ Econ 135(1):169–190
Graham JR, Grennan J, Harvey CR, Rajgopal S (2021) Corporate culture: evidence from the field. In: 27th Annual Conference on Financial Economics and Accounting Paper, Columbia Business School Research Paper No. 16-49, Duke I&E Research Paper No. 2016-33. Available at SSRN: https://ssrn.com/abstract=2805602
Guiso L, Sapienza P, Zingales L (2015) The value of corporate culture. J Financ Econ 117(1):60–76
Hanaeda H, Sasaki T, Suzuki K (2020). Corporate culture in Japanese firms: a survey analysis (in Japanese). In: Hanaeda H, Serita T, Peng X, Sasaki T, Suzuki K, Sasaki T. *Nihon no Corporate Finance: Survey data niyoru bunseki* (Corporate finance in Japan: Analyses based on survey data), HAKUTO-SHOBO Publishing
Haneda S, Ito K (2018) Organizational and human resource management and innovation: which management practices are linked to product and/or process innovation? Res Policy 47(1):194–208
Hartmann M, Hassan A (2006) Application of real options analysis for pharmaceutical R&D project valuation: empirical results from a survey. Res Policy 35(3):343–354
Hellman T, Thiele V (2011) Incentives and innovation: a multitasking approach. Am Econ J Microecon 3(1):78–128
Holmström B (1989) Agency costs and innovation. J Econ Behav Organ 12(3):305–327
Holmström B, Milgrom P (1991) Multitask principal-agent analyses: incentive contracts, asset ownership, and job design. J Law Econ Organ 7(Special Issue):24–52.
Hullova D, Simms CD, Trott P, Laczko P (2019) Critical capabilities for effective management of complementarity between product and process innovation: cases from the food and drink industry. Res Policy 48(1):339–354
Kaplan SN, Strömberg P (2003) Financial contracting theory meets the real world: an empirical analysis of venture capital contracts. Rev Econ Stud 70(2):281–315
Kastl J, Martimort D, Piccolo S (2013) Delegation, ownership concentration and R&D spending: evidence from Italy. J Ind Econ 61(1):84–107
Kreps DM (1997) Intrinsic motivation and extrinsic motivation. Am Econ Rev 87(2):359–364
Krieger J, Li D, Papanikolaou D (2022) Missing novelty in drug development. Rev Financ Stud 35(2):636–679
Laursen KL, Foss NJ (2003) New human resource management practices, complementarities and the impact on innovation performance. Camb J Econ 27:243–263
Manso G (2011) Motivating innovation. J Finance 66(5):1823–1860
Mao Y, Tian X, Yu X (2014) Unleashing innovation. Mimeo
March JG (1991) Exploration and exploitation in organizational learning. Organ Sci 2(1):71–87

References

Onishi K (2013) The effects of compensation plans for employee inventions on R&D productivity: new evidence from Japanese panel data. Res Policy 42(2):367–378

Onishi K, Owan H, Nagaoka S (2021) How do inventors respond to financial incentives? Evidence from the unanticipated court decision on employees' inventions in Japan. J Law Econ 64(2):301–339

Ono A, Haneda S, Ikeda Y, Inui T (2020) The current status of R&D management practices and innovations in Japan (in Japanese). NISTEP Discussion Paper No. 189

O'Reilly C, Chatman JA (1996) Culture as social control: corporations, cults, and commitment. In: Staw BM, Cummings LL (eds) Research in organizational behavior, vol 18. JAI Press, Greenwich, CT, pp 157–200

Prendergast C (1999) The provision of incentives in firms. J Econ Lit 37(1):7–63

Prendergast C (2002) The tenuous trade-off between risk and incentives. J Polit Econ 110(5):1071–1102

Prendergast C (2011) What have we learnt about pay for performance? Economic and Social Review 42(2):113–134

Sahlman WA (1990) The structure and governance of venture-capital organizations. J Financ Econ 27(2):473–521

Sauermann H, Cohen WM (2010) What makes them tick? Employee motives and firm innovation. Manage Sci 56(12):2134–2153

Smolnik T, Bergmann T (2020) Structuring and managing the new product development process: review on the evolution of the Stage-Gate process. J Bus Chem 17(1):41–57

Teece DJ (1996) Firm organization, industrial structure, and technological innovation. J Econ Behav Organ 31(2):193–224

Thakor AJ (2016) Corporate culture in banking. FRBNY Economic Policy Review Issue, August, 5–16

Tian X (2011) The causes and consequences of venture capital stage financing. J Financ Econ 101(1):132–159

Tian X, Wang TY (2014) Tolerance for failure and corporate innovation. Rev Financ Stud 27(1):211–255

Wang S, Zhou H (2004) Staged financing in venture capital: moral hazard and risks. J Corp Finan 10(1):131–155

Yung C (2019) Entrepreneurial manipulation with staged financing. J Bank Finance 100:273–282

The manufacturer's authorised representative in the EU is Springer Nature Customer Service Centre GmbH, Europaplatz 3, 69115 Heidelberg, Germany. If you have any concerns regarding our products, please contact ProductSafety@springernature.com

Printed and bound by CPI Group (UK) Ltd, Croydon, CR0 4YY

25/03/2026

02078172-0017